Nine Guiding Principles for Women in Higher Education

T0308372

NINE GUIDING PRINCIPLES

PRINCIPLES

for Women in
Higher Education

KARYN Z. SPROLES

JOHNS HOPKINS UNIVERSITY PRESS | *Baltimore*

Johns Hopkins University Press
2715 North Charles Street
Baltimore, Maryland 21218-4363
www.press.jhu.edu

Library of Congress Cataloging-in-Publication Data
Names: Sproles, Karyn Z., 1961– author.
Title: Nine guiding principles for women in higher education / Karyn Z. Sproles.
Description: Baltimore : Johns Hopkins University Press, 2022. |
Includes bibliographical references and index.
Identifiers: LCCN 2021063008 | ISBN 9781421444963 (paperback) |
ISBN 9781421444970 (ebook)
Subjects: LCSH: Women college teachers—Vocational guidance—United States. |
Women college administrators—Vocational guidance—United States.
Classification: LCC LB2332.32 .S67 2022 | DDC 378.1/2082—dc23/eng/20220124
LC record available at https://lccn.loc.gov/2021063008

A catalog record for this book is available from the British Library.

Special discounts are available for bulk purchases of this book. For more information,
please contact Special Sales at specialsales@jh.edu.

CONTENTS

PREFACE

How to Thrive in Higher Education

When I started this preface, it was mid-May 2020, in the midst of the COVID-19 pandemic. My colleagues and I in the English Department at the United States Naval Academy had been sheltering in place for more than eight weeks. In mid-March, we had moved classes online and, a few months later, would attend a virtual graduation. Our annual three-day conference on teaching and learning turned into an entire week of online workshops about teaching online. We had no idea what would happen in the fall. All the unknowns were driving us nuts.

We have had to get used to holding classes online or teaching in masks. We are concerned that struggling institutions won't survive the ongoing pandemic. We worry about our colleagues and graduate students facing what will undoubtedly be a bleak job market. The biggest unknown is how COVID-19 will alter higher education as we know it. Changes in the nature and structure of colleges and universities have been a long time coming. Especially at risk is the small liberal arts college—the symbolic embodiment of the traditional higher education paradigm. Such schools were the long-held fantasy for mostly white, uber-privileged as well as semi-privileged middle-class 18- to 22-year-old students, typically envisioned as staying up to the wee hours of the morning on residential campuses, engaged in heartfelt discussions about the meaning of life and the definition of beauty. Indeed, this was largely fantasy. Higher education can no longer ignore the changes that have already occurred, and those changes will likely accelerate in the years to come. One thing that has been slow to change is the number of women in leadership roles. We need more women university presidents, provosts, deans, and department chairs. Women's leadership is crucial in shaping the future of higher education.

The time has arrived for a deep critique of academia's competitive, elitist, reification of privilege, and Kathleen Fitzpatrick's brilliant book *Generous Thinking: A Radical Approach to Saving the University* does just that. Fitzpatrick argues, "However much we as scholars might reject individualism as part and parcel of the humanist, positivist ways of the past, our working lives—on campus and off—are overdetermined by it . . . This competitive individualism contradicts—and in fact undermines all of the most important communal aspects of life within our institutions of higher education" (26-27). This, Fitzpatrick reasons, prevents faculty members from making the case that education is a public—not just an individual—good. I look forward to more critiques of the fundamental flaws in the structure of American higher education, and I take heart in Fitzpatrick's call for us to work together to build new models. I hope that at the center of the new vision we collectively create is a determination to help each other thrive.

While *Nine Guiding Principles for Women in Higher Education* is more practical than theoretical, it is founded on principles of generosity described by Fitzpatrick. It imagines higher education in which collaboration, trust, and a shared vision of mutual success combine to foster an environment in which everyone can thrive. I have created nine principles designed to support women within the current structure, but to also provide a template for changing that structure into one in which competition, animosity, disillusionment, and resentment are diminished. I deal with this idea explicitly in Principle 9, but the entire book is a call to transform higher education. Following these principles will allow you to thrive and in turn contribute to a revitalized culture of higher education that realizes the intellectual community that I believe we all seek.

I've learned an enormous amount lately, though mostly things I never wanted to know, like how to make synchronous online classes interactive—Duh! Small groups. In my department at the Naval Academy, we function like a small liberal arts college, but with a focus on STEM (science, technology, engineering, and math). We are not tuition driven, but the budget has been static for several years, and travel, which had been restricted because of budgets, is now additionally hampered by COVID-19. Nevertheless, we are fortunate: we don't face closure like some schools will as the result of pandemic-driven loses in revenue and lower enrollment. In fact, until now, we haven't had to confront dramatic change. Instead, I have been constantly surprised in pleasant ways.

My colleagues have outdone themselves in pivoting to online teaching, and with that came one happy surprise: We agree that we have become better teachers as a result. Even when we go back to face-to-face classes, we'll continue to use the skills and technologies we've recently learned. Moving the teaching and learning conference online led to higher attendance. One session included 95 participants; the previous year, it had thrilled me that half that number attended the opening keynote. Even more surprising was that the online format produced more interactivity: People shared resources. The chat room was in constant use. People asked questions, answers poured in. We filmed every session, so we now have that as an archival resource. People have been mining the chats for ideas and links.

There was another surprise. I typically have about a dozen faculty members sign up for a preparing for promotion and tenure workshop. This year 28 registered for the first online version. I had organized the materials online and discovered what so many of my colleagues already knew: online instruction reaches more people, and even though there is a large upfront cost in time, it is a one-time expenditure. It took a pandemic for us to make such a change. The time has now come for more than minor adjustments.

We need to rethink higher education, but this time white women and BIPOC (Black, Indigenous, people of color) faculty need to be part of—indeed, need to lead—in shaping this new vision for academia. How can we really serve all of the people who desire a higher education? How can we inspire those who don't yearn for one? How can higher education be made affordable and sustainable? The purpose of this book is not to answer these questions, but to serve as a call to action for those of us who can.

So many of the books and articles I've read of late are about "surviving" in higher education. I want you to do more than survive. I want you to thrive. The nine principles discussed in this book will help you do that. They are all about overcoming the obstacles in your path—and yes, there are real obstacles—so you can find joy and satisfaction in academia.

This is a book I hope you will keep on your desk or your nightstand to dip into at any time in your life in higher education. The chapters are roughly chronological, from your first job through leadership opportunities, providing guidance from the beginning of your career and on into future leadership roles. Maybe this book will actually inspire you to transform higher education by taking on a leadership role.

The book is addressed to women, with special attention to BIPOC women, because we women have particular issues that can get in the way of our success as academics. I keep in the forefront of my mind that women in higher education have complex identities, among them BIPOC, white, international, straight, LGBTQ+, nonbinary, young, middle-aged, senior, disabled, able-bodied (for now), parent, and caregiver to parents and other family members. This is just a short list of identities that our colleagues may or may not be aware. We are or represent a myriad of different positions—such as graduate students, adjuncts, limited-term appointees, and tenure-track, tenured, and full professors as well as administrators or staff in writing, teaching, and research centers, community colleges, and private and public universities, among others. This book will be useful for women in all and more of these situations while also realizing that our roles will likely change over the course of our careers.

The book is also for men who mentor or simply interact with their female colleagues. It can give them insight into the difficulties women have as we manage teaching, research, and life generally. I think it will also be particularly useful to BIPOC men, who may share some of the challenges women face in trying to fit into a culture dominated by white men. It is also a book that teaching centers can use in helping women become oriented to academic life. As the director of USNA's

Center for Teaching and Learning, it is the book I have been looking for. It is a book I would give to all new female faculty and also use for a book group; the nine principles would work perfectly for a monthly book group during the academic year since there is a principle for every month. I currently read Robert Boice's wonderful *Advice for New Faculty Members* with our new faculty, but it's starting to feel a bit dated in insufficiently addressing the concerns of women, especially BIPOC women.

How Does This Book Work?

Nine Guiding Principles can be read as a whole, but each chapter stands alone to allow readers to dip into issues on their minds at any given time. The chapters are deliberately concise, synthesizing the current literature on the topic at hand. Chapters end with a succinct list of actions you can take and a few books to read if you want to learn more. Throughout, I draw heavily from my own experience of nearly 40 years as an academic—from graduate teaching assistant through promotion and tenure and on to department chair, dean, and provost. I have tried to write in a conversational tone, and it is my hope that experiences my colleagues and I have had will add flesh to the research.

I am fortunate to have had colleagues willing to share their experiences with me and who gave me permission to tell their stories here. I am particularly grateful to the BIPOC female academics who generously provided me insight into their specific challenges. As a white woman, I can listen and advocate for change even if I cannot know exactly what it feels like to suffer the systemic racial oppression I sadly recognize in higher education. In each chapter, I go beyond anecdote and advice to try to gain and share insight into the structures that create challenges for us so that we can better navigate the path to success. One of the messages that permeates this book is this: you are not alone.

The paths to success for women, especially BIPOC women, in higher education are rockier than the paths paved for our white male colleagues. When I first started teaching, my friends and I were equally affirmed and disheartened when in 1982 the Association of American Colleges' Project on the Status and Education of Women published Roberta Hall and Bernice Sandler's "The Classroom Climate: A Chilly One for Women?" It wasn't just us, we discovered. Higher education really is a hard place for all women. It's certainly getting better though. There are more of us, for one thing. There are still fewer women in positions of power than I would like to see, however, and I think part of the reason for that is the difficulty of the day-to-day for women in higher education. I hope this book will make every day less of a struggle and more of a joy.

Speaking of joy, this book would not have been possible, and it certainly would not have been so joyful, without my wonderful early readers. Unending thanks to Sharika Crawford, Susan Facknitz, Jaye Falls, Samara Firebaugh, Elizabeth Kendall, Amy Ksir, Irene Lietz, Beth Littleton, Adela Penagos, Silvia Peart, Daphne Skipper, and to the members of the 2019–20 Naval Academy Boice Reading Group: Brielle Harbin, Tori Johnson, Carolyn Judge, Liliana Velasquez Montoya, Anna Svirsko, Anna Wargula, and Jane Wessel. Thanks also to the faculty who tested the 4 Sproles Tests of Education (4 STEP) Quiz in Principle 8: Gabriel Bloomfield, Hezi Brosh, Matthew Buck, William Casey, Ana Contreras, Rob Curry, Jen Flemming, Matthew Fronk, Liz Getto, Katie Hogan, Scott Hottovy, Kathleen Hudson, Mee Song Im, Michelle Jamer, Paola Jarramillo Cienfuegos, Tori Johnson, Carolyn Judge, Irene Lietz, Jamie Lomax, Andrew Metzer, Van Nguyen, Judith Rosenstein, Michael Sanders, Robert Saunders, Aisatta Sidikou, Anna Svirsko, Matt Testerman, Kate Thompson, Anna Wargula, Jane Wessel, Shirley Wong, Oskar Zorilla, and the 140 students leading the Midshipman Group Study Program.

I am grateful to everyone who allowed me to quote our personal emails and conversations throughout these pages. Thank you for giving me permission to include your voices in this book.

Nine Guiding Principles for Women in Higher Education

PRINCIPLE 1

Face Down Impostor Syndrome

I WENT TO COLLEGE EARLY and then straight to graduate school. In English departments, where there were few if any research assistants, it was common to assign funded graduate students their own section of freshman composition to teach. I was 21 when I taught my first freshman composition class. Talk about feeling like an impostor. This was Buffalo in the early 1980s, just after the fall of Bethlehem Steel and when supporting plants were shutting down. As a result, half of the class consisted of thoroughly disgruntled middle-aged white men who had just been laid off from the cardboard box factory. After I went through the syllabus, one of them raised his hand and asked, "How long have *you* been teaching?" I looked at my watch and answered, "About 10 minutes."

I didn't realize it at the time, but I had impostor syndrome—the feeling that you are not the expert even though you are in the position of one. It emerges when you feel judged or, in my case, when I was actually being judged. Clearly, the intellectual authority cultivated by my mostly male undergraduate professors was not a model that would work for me, so I showed the class that there was something I could teach them that they needed to learn—how to write.

Every day I presented a prompt, after which we had five minutes to write. We then passed around what we had written. I use "we" deliberately because I wrote too. I didn't do this to prove a point. I was simply motivated by the idea that I shouldn't ask them to do anything I wasn't willing to do myself. I knew that the more you write, the better you write, so I figured that if nothing else I could get them to write more. As it turned out, when they saw that I wrote three times as much as they did, they quickly understood that I had something to teach them. Finding a way to be authentic in the classroom allayed my self-created and overtly reinforced impostor syndrome until I built up the experience that I needed to actually feel confident in the classroom (most of the time).

I thought of this recently when a new faculty member asked at the beginning of her first semester, "How do I walk into class and present myself as an expert?" The implication was clear: she didn't feel like an expert. That's impostor syndrome. In such a case, rather than overcompensating or being defensive, the answer might be to find, as I did, a new model for what it means to stand in front of a group of students who might not be much younger than you. When I first started teaching, I didn't resent the need to prove myself. Who was I to be teaching in the first place? I now recognize that my students have no idea who I am, so when I introduce myself to the class on the first day, I try to give them some idea of me as a person. I tell them I started teaching college classes in 1982 and that I've written a couple of books. I also throw in a bit about my path to my current position. I've learned along the way that you don't have to know everything about a subject to be capable of teaching it, so I explain to them why I'm passionate about what we'll be studying together.

A friend of mine once said, "Father doesn't know best; he just knows more." You need to be confident enough to say, "That's a great question. Let me think about that." Then you need to find the answer and start the next class talking about it. Tell the class how you found it. In doing so, you're modeling what it is to be engaged, curious, and resourceful. This might not be enough, however, to keep you from feeling like a fraud.

In *Generous Thinking*, an extraordinary analysis of higher education's failure to make itself relevant, Kathleen Fitzpatrick argues that the culture of competition in academia pushes us to try to top one another rather than to deeply listen and try to understand our colleagues' research. I think this competitive culture contributes to the widespread feelings of inadequacy and fear experienced by so many academics. Impostor syndrome makes you feel like you don't belong, like you can't compete. You believe you have no right to be in the position you have earned, and with that feeling comes the fear that you will be found out. Nearly every academic feels this way. That's why you'll regularly find articles on the subject in the *Chronicle of Higher Education*. They're an excellent source for help in combatting this feeling of inadequacy.

Even if you have never experienced impostor syndrome, it is important to know that you are likely surrounded by colleagues who have it. The feeling is real even though it may seem absurd. Our credibility is based on our intellectual authority, so it's no wonder that the fear of not being seen as smart enough emerges when we feel like our very intelligence is being judged. Women are especially susceptible to this feeling. In fact, impostor syndrome was first identified by the psychotherapists Pauline Clance and Suzanne Imes while working with groups of high-achieving female academics. BIPOC women are particularly at risk of experiencing anxiety due to feeling like they don't belong.

There is plenty of advice out there on impostor syndrome. W. Brad Johnson and David G. Smith, authorities on mentoring, recommend that mentors working with colleagues suffering from impostor syndrome point out the facts: you were hired because the committee believed that you are right for the job and that you can succeed at it. Talking to a mentor, or better yet a peer, is an excellent idea. It's likely he or she will be able to not only commiserate, but to also affirm to you your value to the department. A mentor can assure you that you belong. One of the features of impostor syndrome is the urge to hide what you believe is your inadequacy, if you expose this feeling— share it with others—it quickly becomes clear that it has no basis in reality. Hiding it only perpetuates it. All these gestures will feel good, but what causes us to feel like impostors in the first place and why is this feeling so hard to shake even in the face of evidence to the contrary?

An explanation of this tenacious feeling of not belonging can be found in psychologist Claude Steele's work on the unconscious internalizations of stereotypes, such as that women aren't good at math or that BIPOC people aren't smart. Even when we do not share these ridiculous opinions, part of us knows that we live in a society that too often does. We have all had experiences like my first day teaching freshman comp, when the prejudice that young women have no authority in the classroom was exposed. Such incidents, Steele shows, lead women to unconsciously feel anxiety to *not* prove the stereotype correct. In *Whistling Vivaldi: How Stereotypes Affect Us and What We Can Do*, Steele describes his career-long research on identity contingencies or, as Steele explains,

> the things you have to deal with in a situation because you have a given social identity, because you are old, young, gay, a white male, a woman, black, Latino, politically conservative or liberal, diagnosed with bipolar disorder, a cancer patient, and so on. Generally speaking, contingencies are circumstances you have to deal with in order to get what you want or need in a situation. In the Chicagoland of my youth, in order to go swimming I had to restrict my pool going to Wednesday afternoons [when Blacks were allowed to use the otherwise whites-only pool]. That's a contingency. (3–4)

I hope you can see how stereotype threat plays into and exacerbates impostor syndrome by creating culturally constructed judgements about the intelligence of women and BIPOC faculty. Even when we don't start out feeling like impostors, we still might feel that we have to prove we aren't. And that raises the fear that we might be.

Steele takes the title of his book from an anecdote he tells about Brent Staples, an African American who as a graduate student would whistle Vivaldi as he walked home from the University of Chicago to signal that he wasn't a threat to anyone. Steele wrote,

People from other groups in other situations might face very different stereotypes—about lacking math ability rather than being violence prone for example—but their predicaments would be the same. When they were in situations where those stereotypes could apply to them, they understood that one false move could cause them to be reduced to that stereotype, to be seen and treated in terms of it. That's stereotype threat, a contingency of their identity in these situations. (6–7)

Steele and his colleagues conducted study after study to determine the influence of stereotype threat in our lives. They discovered that the often-unconscious anxiety that women feel when taking math tests resulted in their not doing as well as their suggested ability in low-stakes, math-related situations. Steele had earlier done experiments in which men and women undergraduates with similar scores in math were given math tests from the Graduate Record Exam. They were not prepped for the material, and the test was deliberately chosen to create anxiety and frustration. The women got significantly lower scores. To test whether this the result stemmed from the women's increased anxiety due to stereotype threat, students in a subsequent repetition of the experiment were first told, "'You may have heard that women don't do as well as men on difficult standardized math tests, but . . . on this *particular* test, women always do as well as men'" (38; emphasis in original). In this case, the women did indeed do just as well as the men. Steele conducted many more experiments to elicit and then negate stereotype threat, creating a body of work demonstrating the threat's power to induce stress and anxiety strong enough to diminish performance. (See "Workshops" for a list of strategies derived from Steele's work that can help mitigate stereotype threat in the classroom.)

Feeling like an impostor is what happens when stereotype threat shifts from an unconscious to a conscious feeling of being judged that is detrimental to performance. If you are a BIPOC woman in a STEM field, the contingencies abound, including not having many (or any) colleagues who look like you to having students who test your mettle. One of my colleagues, who identifies as Black, told me that a white female student had dismissed her feedback on an assignment by telling her, "You're not a real engineer." I think we can be fairly certain that the student wouldn't have said such a thing to a white male engineering professor. As Sindhumathi Revuluri notes in "How to Overcome Impostor Syndrome," "Some academics don't just feel like impostors, they are *made* to feel like impostors . . . You may find, as I did, that your own feelings of being an impostor are related to that implicit definition of who belongs in your field and on campus—and not to your scholarship, teaching, or citizenship."

The anxiety and stress of impostor syndrome can negatively affect your productivity and even your health. In explaining why Black women in Fresno, California, experience infant mortality at three times the national rate of white women, sociologist Whitney N. Lester Pirtle wrote, "Ample research has shown that this disparity is not due to genetics or social class but is the result of stress accumulation, based on race and gender, over the life course" (4). Heath problems in many other regards are more common and more serious among Black adults. You can find current data on health disparities in annual reports published by the National Center for Health Statistics.

Impostor syndrome and stereotype threat, along with the stress they induce, are real. They are not a sign of weakness or lack of preparedness or ability. What they do show is that we care deeply about what we are doing and want to succeed at it—feelings not to be ashamed of. After all, aren't they what drew us to higher education in the first place? We cannot control who has been hired before us or the prejudices (often unconscious) that students bring into the classroom, but we can address the feeling of being an impostor that they trigger. We need to do this to be productive and also to remain healthy.

Many women who told me their thoughts about being an imposter said that they just didn't feel like experts. They worried that they would make a mistake in class or wouldn't be able to answer students' questions. It's likely that both of these things will happen, but that shouldn't undermine the years of work it took you to get where you are. Clance and Imes describe it as the "internal experience of [being] intellectual phonies" (1). Who am I to be writing this article? Who am I to be teaching this class? When I first started teaching, I had a recurring vision of someone bursting into my classroom, and with finger pointed, declaring, "What gives you the right to teach Chaucer!" A small part of me worried that I wasn't experienced enough to teach Chaucer, but an even bigger part of me worried that someone was sure I wasn't. Now I hear a voice asking, "Who are you to tell women how to thrive in higher education?"

I don't know you, but I know one thing: As far as knowing your material goes, you've got this. There are many reasons that women struggle in higher education (and we'll get to them), but not knowing your field is almost never one of those reasons. Yet that is the greatest fear expressed by the new faculty I work with each year.

As the title of this chapter suggests, we need to face down impostor syndrome. That means acknowledging it, recognizing that it feels awful, and confronting its origins in past criticisms and uncertainties that are so easily internalized that they have come to define us. You need to do this not just because impostor syndrome makes you feel terrible, but also because it compromises your ability to be successful. It truly is a self-fulfilling prophecy. Just as the stress produced by stereotype threat causes women to underperform, its most potent form, impostor syndrome, triggers a "fixed mindset" that prevents you from learning how to improve. In *Mindset: The New Psychology of Success*, Carol Dweck contrasts "fixed mindset" with "growth mindset." According to her, "When people believe in fixed traits, they are always in danger of being measured by a failure. It can define them in a permanent way. Smart or talented as they may be, this mindset seems to rob them of their coping resources" (39). With a fixed mindset, you don't believe you can improve; you are as smart as you are ever going to be. Thus, you must always perform perfectly. Making a mistake or not being able to answer a question in class feels like the end of the world. As Dweck notes, "You have to be flawless right away" (24). With a fixed mindset, everything becomes a test, and no matter how many tests you pass, there is always another one waiting to judge you lacking. There is no pleasure in measuring up, because you know that you will continue to be measured. The judgment that surrounds a fixed mindset is relentless.

Dweck points to new graduate students at Columbia University in her home department, psychology, as an example of how the fixed mindset clamps down when people are faced with a fear of failure: "It took one day for some of them to feel like complete imposters. Yesterday they were hotshots; today they're failures. Here's what happens. They look at the faculty with our long list of publications. 'Oh my God, I can't do that' . . . They know how to take tests and get A's but they don't know how to do *this*—yet. They forget the *yet*" (25; emphasis in original).

This puts me in mind of many of the new faculty we hire at the Naval Academy who worry that making a mistake in class will expose them as the frauds they fear they are. I suspect this feeling is an ongoing one; it certainly can come raging at critical points in research, while going up for tenure or promotion, and especially when taking up a leadership position. A fixed mindset makes us vulnerable to every little criticism or mistake because it's all or nothing. If we aren't perfect in every way, then we really don't belong. Not only that, a fixed mindset shuts down creative problem solving, which is vitally important in the classroom and in research. It makes it hard to productively take on feedback. Everything feels personal and impossible. Doing the things you know you need to do will be that much more difficult if you are struggling with the phantom of your own failure. You can't perform to the best of your ability. You find it impossible to dismiss that nagging sense of doom. I know it is hard work, but you need to take it on.

I had not initially thought of impostor syndrome as being connected to the pitfalls of the fixed mindset, but I think this might be the key. I know I fight against a fixed mindset when I am anxious and stressed, in other words, afraid of failing. I notice that this state makes creative problem solving almost impossible. I go round and round, hitting up against the same roadblocks without making progress. I feel stuck and frustrated. I also see this in faculty who have experienced disappointment in promotions or publications. They can't let go of the failure or see it as an indication that they need to do something differently. Instead, they find something—or usually someone else—to blame.

If your self-worth is tied up in being perfect, the great fear that you are not, and that you will be exposed for the impostor you fear you are, can be overwhelming. It makes it difficult to navigate a new job, a committee assignment, review processes, or even class when you are filled with fear of failure. As Dweck writes: "In the fixed mindset, everything is about the outcome. If you fail—or if you're not the best— it's all been wasted. The growth mindset allows people to value what they're doing *regardless of the outcome*. They're tackling problems, charting new courses, working on important issues" (48; emphasis in original). A fixed mindset goes hand in hand with impostor syndrome. I have certainly experienced this intellectual clampdown.

The daily decision of what to wear is one of the issues that triggers my impostor syndrome. Deborah Tannen's *You're Wearing That?* offers insightful analysis on this particular topic. One indication that your fixed mindset has been triggered is when you go down a rabbit hole of doubt and self-blame. I imagine criticism about my outfit before I even get dressed. Is my skirt too short? Are my trousers too tight? I've been triggered. I hear that little voice that judges me on my appearance. I failed that test again.

My closet is filled with clothes I will never wear again because of the comment here or there that made me feel self-conscious. A colleague confided in me that she wears only earth tones because a male colleague noticed that her clothes were "colorful." She wondered, "Did he say that because I'm a Black woman?" This is clearly a loaded example, because women *are* judged on our appearance—just as I was when I first started teaching. Don't get me wrong, men are judged as well. A white male colleague told me that his colleagues teased him when he wore orange slacks, but there was no evidence that it shook his confidence or changed their opinion of him. He was wearing the slacks when he told me the story. Whereas for women, how we dress is a much more difficult issue, because many of us know from experience that judgment has real consequences. Examples probably aren't necessary, but here are a few: during my promotion and tenure review, a white female colleague questioned my qualifications because I was a "flashy dresser"; a white female colleague referred to one of our new colleagues as the one "who dresses like a little girl"; two Black female colleagues told me they had individually been told by white male colleagues that they were making a political statement when they stopped straightening their hair.

I'm willing to bet that you have plenty of examples of your own. It's exhausting, isn't it? When I start to feel defensive and begin blaming myself or others, I know I need to take a breath. I need to remind myself that a criticism or a failure doesn't define me. It doesn't mean that I'm not capable or smart. If I don't interrogate that moment, however, I get stuck feeling incompetent in every aspect of my life.

To trigger me, no one has to actually say anything about how I dress. I've so internalized that critical voice that I can deploy it all by myself. Packing for a conference used to be almost paralyzing, so sure was I that I would be inappropriately dressed. That internalized critical voice had robbed me of my confidence to recognize that I know full well what it means to look professional. I also realized that I was stressing about my wardrobe to avoid the real anxiety of delivering a paper because the audience would discover that I was a pretender. Impostor syndrome triggered my fixed mindset so that instead of prepping to deliver the paper, I fretted about my shoes. I saw no possibility of improving my delivery, only of being judged poorly and failing. I still have anxiety dreams about packing and finding myself in mismatched outfits.

The internalized voices that make me doubt my teaching and research are even stronger than those involving clothing. As a result, I have learned that I need to fight the tendency to ignore them and just push on through. I can ignore the voices, but it's hard and brings little pleasure. I want to enjoy teaching and research, but to do that, I need to listen to the critical voice and confront it: Where is it coming from? Is it pointing to a worry I can address? Do I just need to counter it?

The research that Barbara Frederickson presents in *Positivity* holds that every negative thought can be overcome by three positive thoughts. Subsequent research has questioned the specificity of her 3:1 ratio, but I find it a handy way to launch the battle against the critical voices that discourage me. Now instead of obsessing about my outfit, I read the paper to a trusted colleague to give me honest feedback, and when I'm packing, I tell myself, "You know how to do this. You have gotten feedback. You have practiced."

Dweck makes the crucial point that our fixed mindset is a version of ourselves we have created to "protect [us] and keep [us] safe. But it has developed some very limiting ways of doing that" (260), such as focusing on what clothes to pack rather than practicing reading a conference paper. This fixed version of ourselves might have developed at a very young age to gain us the approval of a teacher or parent (235). Dweck urges us to "embrace [our] fixed mindset" (254) so we can help transform it into a growth mindset. She even suggests naming it. Mine is Myles, and he comes out when I am around judgmental people because I am terrified of being judged and rejected. Even if these judgy people aren't criticizing me at the moment, I fear they soon will be. Myles is so paralyzed with fear, he can't even think of anything to say. He is stiff, and words don't come easily to him. He plows ahead with plans even when they are clearly not working. He ignores problems and puts his head down, soldiering on out of the need to complete a task.

Presumably there was once some reward for this behavior. This reminds me of first grade, when I so wanted to please my teacher, Miss Fisher, but thought I couldn't. We had been given piles of worksheets to complete, so she could meet with small reading groups while everyone else colored or did connect the dots. I could never finish all the worksheets and felt like a failure every single day. Of course, we were never meant to finish them, their point being to keep us occupied. I'm sure she worked hard to find things for us to do that she thought would be fun as well as educational, but I was trying to please her by completing the task. I failed to enjoy the worksheets or learn anything from them. Part of me still trudges along when I shut down, as with the worksheets, just completing the task to complete it. I stop trying to learn anything. I must say that this trait comes in handy during some stressful situations, such as moving, but it is less than ideal when I'm trying to solve a difficult problem that I am not confident I can solve.

These days, I work on getting Myles to embrace challenges. I know he can do it! I have enlisted a colleague to help me identify those moments when Myles starts to take the wheel and steer. One day I told her about a moment from a workshop that was bothering me. She asked me, "What brought Myles to the table?" Aha. I realized that I felt I was being judged. In this way, I am also trying to educate Myles instead of ignoring him. It is going to be difficult, but I can already feel his foot easing off the brake. When that happens, I can face my fear of not looking like a professional and think about what I want to look like. I can recognize and reject the stereotypes I have internalized about what it means to be a professor and define the role for myself. If I can find a way to bring my authentic self to the classroom or a conference or a department meeting, then I am not an impostor anymore. If we think of the challenges that face us in academia as opportunities for learning and growth—rather than a series of tests that will determine our intrinsic value—I think we are more likely to succeed, enjoy our success, and appreciate the hard work that led to it. Indeed, one of the characteristics of the growth mindset is enjoying a challenge, which in turn produces "perseverance and resilience," two qualities that greatly contribute to success (Dweck 12).

This leads us to Robert Boice's *Advice for New Faculty Members*, which I will refer to a lot. Do yourself a favor and go read it now, but here's my summary: Calm down. Seriously. His research is clear about what leads some faculty to succeed and others to fail, and it isn't for the reasons that make us feel like impostors. Instead, it is for reasons we can control—if we calm down. Boice's research compares faculty who thrive with faculty who struggle. What, he asks, do successful faculty do that faculty who struggle don't do? He concluded,

> Almost all the failures and miseries of these new hires owed to misunderstandings about effective ways of working and socializing. *Never, in my close observations of over a thousand novice professors, did I see someone*

falter for reasons of inexpertise in his or her area of scholarship. Or from lack of desire. Instead, the most telling mistakes were easily correctable problems such as not understanding how to moderate student incivilities in the classroom, not knowing how to manage enough writing for publication in modest amounts of time, and not learning how to elicit effective collegial support. (1; emphasis added)

Boice's book unpacks each of these problems and presents data to back up his findings and recommendations. Each year, I read it with new faculty, slowly, a chapter a week for the entire year. This is a very Boice way to go about it. One of his most important messages is to work at teaching and research in what he calls brief daily sessions. This is advice I have found applicable in nearly every aspect of my life. There will be more on this throughout the book. I cannot recommend Boice's book enough. Senior faculty who've read it at my urging all say they wish they'd read it during their first year of teaching. Each time I've read it (now more than nine times), I find something new to help me through whatever I'm struggling with at the moment, not just in my career, but also in my personal life.

Boice doesn't refer to internalized self-criticism as impostor syndrome, but he warns against criticism that becomes so common we don't realize that the tape playing in the background is whispering negative comments (65–74). This can infuse all parts of the day, from driving to work and searching for parking to prepping for class and teaching to trying to sleep and lying awake. I can hear it now: This exercise isn't going to work; I won't be able to explain this equation; here is where I always make a mistake; no one is going to read my work; nothing in my closet fits anymore. Does this litany sound familiar to you? If so, manage these moments by paying attention to the negative self-talk, asking yourself where the negativity is coming from and then thinking of three positive comments for every negative one. Every time you feel like a fraud is an opportunity to face down your fears and to become better and stronger.

Remember: The department that hired you has a stake in your success. Its committee made the offer because they were convinced you could succeed. They want you to look good because your success makes them look good (regardless of how you dress).

Note to Those Preparing for Leadership Roles

Impostor syndrome often roars with a vengeance when you're preparing to take on a new leadership role. Even as a long-time member of a department, chairing it comes with a steep learning curve. It's great if you have a long and smooth transition with the previous chair, who will likely be delighted to fill you in on everything from important due dates to personnel issues. That is not always the case, however, but even if it is, you should still find a current or previous chair in another department to coach you through the first year. You will be grateful for the objectivity and the support for your sanity. A department chair trying to come up with a fair way to assign offices in anticipation of a move to a new building asked to run her plan by me since I didn't have a stake in situation. I was more than happy to hear the plan and let her talk through the objections she anticipated. She practiced her responses and even came up with an alternative plan to propose that would address the concerns she suspected might arise.

While department chair, one of the things I struggled with was feeling that if I didn't already know how to do something or what to do in a difficult situation, I wasn't adequately prepared to do the job. I felt like I couldn't allow anyone to know that I didn't already know what to do. But here's the thing: Of course I didn't know what to do—yet. No one expects you to know all that a new position entails. Okay, some people will, but they are unrealistic (to put it kindly). Rely on trusted colleagues. If you don't have any, find some, perhaps at another institution. They've been there and will be delighted to guide you.

You have learned how to succeed before. You can learn to do it again.

How to Face Down Impostor Syndrome

- Remember that almost everyone feels like an impostor from time to time.

- Talk to your mentor or other trusted colleagues about this feeling, or if easier, talk to a peer.
- Notice and combat negative self-talking with self-affirmation. As W. Brad Johnson and David G. Smith remind us, you must affirm yourself both as a person and as a professional.
- Recognize your accomplishments. Does everyone have an advanced degree? I don't think so.
- Become conscious of feeling like an impostor and alert to situations in which you feel judged (and in which you are actually being judged).
- Recognize when impostor syndrome encourages a fixed mindset and look out for other situations that trigger a fixed mindset. What precipitates assigning blame?
- Find a way to be authentic in your role.
- Understand that facing down impostor syndrome is hard work and that it never ends. It pops up when you are stretching yourself to do something important.

Want to learn more? I recommend the following:

Boice, Robert. *Advice for New Faculty Members: Nihil Nimus.*
Dweck, Carol. *Mindset: The New Psychology of Success.*
Steele, Claude. *Whistling Vivaldi: How Stereotypes Affect Us and What We Can Do.*

PRINCIPLE 2

Connect with Colleagues

WOMEN, FIND ONE ANOTHER! Connect with colleagues in your department, across the institution, within your discipline. Find allies, create networks, help each other succeed. We need one another. Resist the temptation to hunker down and immerse yourself wholly in your classes and your research.

I get it. I'm an introvert. I'd rather be doing research in my office or prepping for class on my couch, but in the long run, it is the relationships you build that will lead to your success. This is especially true if you are an adjunct or teaching online. Women have a distinct advantage here: Because we are expected to be nurturing and create social ties, let's nurture each other. We need each other to navigate the (still) male-dominated world of higher education. Don't let yourself or each other down by trying to go it alone.

Every Tuesday at noon, I meet with a group of new faculty, mostly women, to talk about Robert Boice's *Advice for New Faculty Members* and their teaching and research experiences. In keeping with Boice's advice to get feedback early on a research project, I asked if they would be willing to read the proposal for this book because they are in part the target audience for the guiding principles. As Boice states, "[Writing's] excessive self-focus keeps us isolated and shy and unlikely to solicit social support—and then overreact . . . to public criticism" (158). I was anxious about sharing the proposal with the group and asking junior colleagues to judge my work. If you've read the previous chapter, you know how I feel about being judged. I was also worried that my request would feel like an imposition.

The group was great. They willingly agreed and gave me valuable feedback. They also asked if they could read the chapters as I drafted them, so you'll be hearing from them again. They especially wanted to talk about social isolation, which Boice says is one of the biggest pitfalls for new faculty: "This shock of social isolation is a key source of stress and disillusionment for brand new faculty" (223). Indeed, everyone chimed in about how lonely the transition to being a new faculty member had been. You typically arrive in the summer to find your future colleagues scattered to the winds. Many come alone, arriving in a new city or town without any social connections. Once the semester begins, you realized that you're at a different stage in life than most members of your department.

My colleagues reminded me of the instant isolation we experience when we move to a new place. When I took my first job in Minnesota, leaving my family and friends behind on the East Coast, I rented a lovely little house on campus with a basement and an attic. I bought a washer and dryer. No more run-down laundromats and having to keep an eagle eye out lest someone steal my clothes (which did happen). It was such a change from constantly worrying about money to going to the grocery store and thinking, "I can buy whatever I want." I felt like I had died and gone to heaven. When I arrived in July, however, the campus had been deserted. Isolation was the only option.

Among all the transitions during that time—going from graduate student to assistant professor, from the East Coast to the Midwest, from penniless to less penniless—I found being alone the most difficult. I had never lived alone, until then. My partner in graduate school had decided at the last minute to take a one-year position elsewhere—and to take the cat with her. I was not even close to beginning to process that. Instead, I was jittery in my new home. I had been trained to feel fearful and vulnerable as a woman alone. Every noise seemed like a potential threat. One night I was reading in the bath when I heard a door open and close. I later realized that the cross-breeze I had deliberately created in the attic—I didn't have air conditioning—periodically blew open and then closed the door to the space. But in the moment, I was certain someone had entered the house. I was frightened, confused, and braced for impact. That's how the first few years felt.

Social isolation is to be expected when you first move to a new place regardless of the stage of your career. The new faculty in my Tuesday reading group pointed out that in college and grad school, they had had a ready-made friends group. When they moved to Annapolis, however, they had to find ways to meet people. Here's a list of their suggestions of places to find friends:

- Gym or yoga studio
- Place of worship or meditation
- Reading groups (try the local library)
- Low-stakes activity groups
  - o Kickball leagues
  - o Ultimate Frisbee clubs
  - o Hiking or biking groups
- Volunteering
- Friendship apps

It is important to develop a social life outside your institution, but this chapter will focus on connecting with colleagues on campus.

Social isolation in academia is, as it sounds, keeping to oneself on campus. This is a habit we often pick up in graduate school, while binge-writing our dissertation. It is tempting to protect ourselves when we are feeling anxious and unsure, but if we don't get occasional feedback on how we're doing, it will probably be too late to make adjustments when we discover that we aren't meeting institutional expectations we didn't even know existed. Keeping to ourselves seems normal, especially if the model is your graduate school professors who only showed up to teach and then headed back to their lab or home office. This is not a practice that leads to a good start or a happy career.

It's for good reason that Boice warns us that social isolation is a key problem that can derail new faculty members. If we don't make connections with our colleagues, we can't expect them to support us during periods of reappointment, promotion, or tenure. If they don't really know us, they won't be invested in our future. Even if we meet the standards for teaching and research, the more nebulous issue of "service" and the often-unwritten expectation of collegiality can be more problematic than we are led to believe. As always, this is especially true for women and all BIPOC faculty.

Boice is refreshingly candid in stating, "My guess about why academe keeps its criteria for socialization and service vague is this: Unstated and uncalibrated rules leave the most control for gatekeepers because they can adjust their implicit criteria to fit their biases" (203). I hope your internal alarm bells are going off. My guess is that the senior faculty who will be making the crucial decisions about your future are not always likely to have a bias toward supporting all women and BIPOC men—yet. Bottom line: if your colleagues like you—translation, look like you—you'll probably succeed. If your colleagues don't like you—or just don't know you very well—you might be surprised by the roadblocks you stand to face.

One of my Black female colleagues asked several people, all white men, for help working out the guidelines for hiring a research assistant; all of whom said they had no idea, when in fact, all of them had hired an assistant in the past. And here's the worst thing about those roadblocks: you might not realize you've been rerouted, because it often happens in the form of not warning you about something or not giving you help with something else. You won't even recognize that you're on a side road until you fail to arrive where you thought you were headed. Someone might not deliberately give you bad directions, but they also might not say, "Stop! That's a dead end."

Cultivating colleagues who can and will volunteer good advice is especially crucial for adjunct faculty members. I know you are likely racing from one class to another, and in some of your cases, driving between institutions to cobble together a full-time job. You should not, however, lose sight of the fact that if your colleagues know you,

you will be more likely to get rehired and have a more accommodating schedule. A friendly interaction doesn't have to take long. I sometimes think the most productive part of my day is chatting around the photocopier. I try to pay attention to the questions my colleagues ask that generate good conversations. "What are you teaching today?" is my favorite. We are always eager to talk about that. On the other hand, "How is your research going?" may very well lead to a deer-in-the-headlights situation.

Connecting with colleagues is probably easier for extroverts, who are naturally friendly and outgoing. For us introverts, it feels more natural to hole up in our offices or labs or living rooms or coffee shops, especially those of us who are also shy. After all, that is when we are getting our work done. Unless we're working collaboratively, we need to be alone to get anything accomplished. I can happily spend weeks on end reading and writing without having a single meaningful conversation. When I've done it, it's been great. I confess that I'm one of the people who was relieved by the required canceling of social engagements to prevent the spread of COVID-19.

Being alone recharges me, and like me, a lot of faculty members tend to be introverts. Academia appeals to us because it is conducive to being alone. I find great solace in Susan Cain's *Quiet: The Power of Introverts in a World That Can't Stop Talking*. It helped me understand the difficulty I have speaking in a group if I don't have a specific role. Teaching isn't a problem in this regard because I'm supposed to be in charge. Similarly, I would rather host a party than attend one. Cain's book is excellent in helping introverts understand the social anxiety that often accompanies introversion. Not all introverts are shy, but many are. I am. I prefer seeing and dealing with people one-on-one. This was an important thing for me to recognize about myself. *Quiet* might be an even more important book for the extroverts among you because it can help you see and understand why your quiet colleagues (and family members) might be silently seething.

Cain points to cultural historian Warren Susman's argument that the current privileging of extroversion resulted from the migration of agricultural laborers to the city in the United States, which transformed American society from a "culture of character" to a "culture of personality": "In the Culture of Character, the ideal self was serious, disciplined, and honorable. What counted was not so much the impression one made in public as how one behaved in private . . . But when they embraced the Culture of Personality, Americans . . . became captivated by people who were bold and entertaining" (21). In cities, your neighbors wouldn't have known your family well enough to know what you did in private. All they had to judge you by was the impression you made. Hence, Cain points out, following Susman, there was a shift in self-help books during the 1920s from "inner virtue to outer charm" (22). That's how we ended up with books like Dale Carnegie's *How to Win Friends and Influence People*, John Molloy's *Dress for Success*, and the many other books on how to be more assertive.

Quiet is enlightening. It is also deeply affirming because Cain points out the many strengths that come with introversion—thoughtfulness, self-reliance, and caution—but also a greater willingness to take a risk if confident of success. But they don't change the fact that in most Western cultures, extroverts are privileged. You don't have to be an extrovert to get to know your colleagues, but you do need to be deliberate about it.

I hope the previous chapter convinced you that you deserve your job and are fully capable of doing it. That said, it is only reasonable to also recognize that there are areas in which you are not an expert. That might be one of the reasons that impostor syndrome is so difficult to shake during your first years in a position: it's more comfortable to worry about a problem you don't have than it is to worry about something you probably should worry about. When you are new on campus, you are not an expert on the department, the institution, or the students you will be teaching. Let's face it. You don't know what you don't know.

It might feel hard to reach out to your colleagues, but you should ask for help. It is a great way to connect with them. Thinking that asking for help is an admission that they aren't qualified for the job often trips up new faculty members; this feeling will likely arise again when they take on new responsibilities or leadership roles. As I've said, you can't possibly know the department and institutional culture and expectations upon arrival. This is especially true if you happen to be at an institution where you were a student. The roles are so different that thinking you totally understand the place can actually get in your way.

More often than not, your colleagues will be flattered if you ask their advice. Don't you love it when people ask you for advice? You feel respected and valued, and so will they. Give them that bit of joy by asking if you can see one of their syllabuses or if they would review one of yours. How much writing and reading should you assign? Do they have a rubric they would be willing to share? Do this by email before you even arrive on campus and especially if you'll be teaching remotely. Reach out to members of the hiring committee or someone working close to your field. Identify potential contacts while interviewing, and while you're at it, ask whether they have time to go for coffee if they're going to be around during the summer, perhaps when you return to house hunt or virtually if you can't meet in person. The department chair and members of the search committee have a vested interest in your success. Stay in touch with them occasionally as you prepare to move, and you will likely find them on hand to give you a warm welcome (even if on Zoom). You won't come off as someone who doesn't know what you're doing. You'll look like someone who is making an effort to do a great job.

Don't forget about the department staff. They are often the best source of information for what's going on in the department and across campus. They will also be instrumental in getting you established and getting you what you need. Be kind and grateful to them at every opportunity. While chair, one of my colleagues made it a point to keep fresh flowers on the desk of the department's administrative assistant. Not only did she appreciate it, we all did. Asking for help shouldn't stop after you've found your feet. Make it an ongoing practice.

Make use of new faculty orientation to network with colleagues from different departments. People often bond at this event. Take the opportunity to act deliberately, and make a plan to meet again for coffee or at a teaching workshop if offered on your campus. Here is a shameless plug for teaching and learning centers: regardless of whether they realize it, their programs offer one of the few ways for faculty to make connections outside of their department aside from committee work. Go to workshops on teaching even if you don't have time and aren't interested in the topic. When people tell me they don't have time for something, I hear "that's not worth my time." Because making social connections is one of the most important things you can do to ensure a successful career, the time you spend on it will pay dividends when you're up for renewal, tenure, or promotion. If some of the people on the committee know you and see you as a good citizen and active member of the intellectual community, they will want you to succeed.

The workings of your department are among some of the things you'll need to learn: Is it standard practice to take a research day, or is everyone expected to be in their office on workdays? Is attendance at faculty meetings mandatory? Consider all department meetings and other institutional gatherings as obligations—including committee meetings, town halls, and graduation networking events—and try not to weigh in on agenda topics until you know where the bodies are buried. If you want to contribute an idea, it might be prudent to mention it to the chair outside of the meeting. Remember that you are likely walking in mid-conversation without knowing what people are *really* talking about.

To get an idea of what might be going on behind the scenes, Read Richard Russo's hysterically funny novel *Straight Man*. Beware that it is set largely in an English department, the events at which might seem exaggerated if you're in a field less given to drama. I'm not saying that it's common for someone to accidentally eavesdrop on a meeting because they're hiding in the ceiling, but it's not as far-fetched as you might think. In your department, it will take a while to figure out the unwritten rules, because to the rest of the department, they are unexamined assumptions that they expect you will share. You don't have to share them, but you need to know what they are.

Back at my Midwest campus, I felt like a solid citizen when I wrote for an hour or two in the morning, got to my office at 9:00 or 10:00 and left at 5:00 or 6:00. I thought it was odd that everyone was gone by 3:00 or so, but I figured they had school buses to meet. It was only after I became chair and started going in at what seemed to me an ungodly hour, to deal with the workload, that I discovered that the rest of the department arrived at 7:00 so they could start the day at 8:00 East Coast time. It was then that collegial socializing occurred. Who knew? I had been missing out on this for years. I'm not sure I would have changed my ways, but at least I would have been making a deliberate choice.

Since many academics tend to be introverts, you might find that your colleagues aren't particularly social. If that's the case, you will have to make an added effort to get to know members of your department and folks outside the department. Google your colleagues. Read their research and ask them about it, but don't offer an unsolicited critique. Look for natural ways to connect: new faculty orientation, workshops, book groups, the faculty lunchroom if there is one. If the opportunities are few, initiate some. Create a writing group in your department or with an affinity group, such as new faculty or BIPOC faculty or LGBTQ+ faculty, or nonbinary faculty. Find a research partner or group for weekly check-ins. Make good use of your mentors, whether you're formally assigned one or you think of someone as a mentor. More on this in the next principle.

I am not suggesting that you become best friends with your colleagues. There is a difference between being friendly and being friends. I would act cautiously in moving from friendly to friendship. I know it sounds like middle school, but there are likely to be people who will not treat you cordially if you become friends with certain other people. You'd be amazed at what grievances, relationships, and possibly even lawsuits had occurred before you arrived. It wasn't until graduation during my first year at a new job that I noticed that the chair of my department and another department weren't speaking. Their spat had been going on so long that no one could remember the cause. As the senior faculty members, they led the procession into graduation. They stood at the front of the line, back-to-back, willing each other out of existence. By now I knew my chair to be a sensitive but vengeful man. It was clear to me in that moment that if I had become friends (or even been friendly) with his archenemy, I wouldn't have been coming back in the fall. It turns out that all those times my chair's nemesis snubbed me, he was actually protecting me.

The lesson here: Learn the lay of the land by developing cordial relationships in the department. This is also important for identifying potential mentors and allies. Once again, this is critical if you are a BIPOC woman and also essential if you are LGBTQ+ and/or nonbinary. In *I'm Still Here: Black Dignity in a World Made for Whiteness*, Austin Channing Brown offers 10 tips under the rubric "How to Survive Racism in an Organization That Claims to Be Antiracist." Tip 7 is "Find your people . . . Build or join an antiracist cohort within the organization" (129). So true.

Building a cohort might be more challenging if you're LGBTQ+. I was talking to a gay white male colleague about the affinity group I was trying to start for LGBTQ+ faculty and staff. He was enthusiastic about the idea, but not for the reason I expected. He said, "That would be great! I would really like to know who the other queer faculty are." I guess people tend to tell me, but my colleague is right that this crucial marker of identity is not always apparent since the dominant assumption is that everyone is straight. My trans friends have a bigger issue here, which, honestly, cries out for a book of its own. Fortunately, there is one: *Being and Becoming Professionally Other: Identities, Voices, and Experiences of U.S. Trans* Academics* by Erich Pitcher. Seek allies by looking up the faculty sponsor for the student LGBTQ+ group or the person who organizes Safe Space or Safe Zone trainings. I organize Safe Space training on campus and am beyond thrilled when faculty attend who are willing to share their stories of coming out or transitioning. These sessions have led to many friendships.

Just as you need to develop an authentic teaching persona, you also need to remain aware of your professional persona. We have all run into people who overshare in the line at the bank or grocery store. Don't be that person. There's a reason people talk about parking and the weather. Resist talking about intimate topics, such as health issues and relationships. You might be an open book, but your colleagues might not be ready for a good read. Talking about teaching is always a safe subject, and I think we should engage each other more often about it. Once you discover which of your colleagues have pets, you'll never lack for a topic of conversation with them.

Look to colleagues in other departments—or better yet people unaffiliated with the institution—for your friendship circle. Still, you'll need to have relationships in the department that are friendly enough so that as Trisalyn Nelson and Jessica Early say in "How to Counter the Isolation of Academic Life," you have "someone who can cover your class at the last minute when your kids start throwing up" (2).

Establish and maintain scholarly networks. Nelson and Early describe such networks as an "ecology—a living breathing, ever-shifting collection of connections and contacts that needs time and attention to nurture and grow" (1). One suggestion they make for gracefully staying in touch with the senior scholars who have supported you is to show your gratitude by nominating them for awards and talking up their work (2). Stay in touch with your graduate school friends and professors, but be careful about taking their advice if they're not at a similar institution. New faculty often tell me that their dissertation directors had advised them to forget research and instead focus on teaching. The Naval Academy is an undergraduate institution with a commitment to teaching, but there are also research expectations that would be difficult to meet if faculty failed to keep it up from the start. Even if research expectations are low, if you let your research slide, it will be hard to pick it back up, and thus difficult to move to another institution should you ever want to do so.

Go to conferences, including virtual ones, and keep in touch with the folks you meet there. Go to the women's caucus lunches and other affinity group meetings, even if you have to pay for these things yourself. Propose a panel for next year. Even if travel funding is limited, you should still invest in your future. Write a "fan letter" to your favorite critic or researcher. Wouldn't you love to get one from someone?

There are so many ways to build connecting with colleagues into daily life without much effort. If you see these opportunities as an investment in your future, it will be easier to slow down and enjoy casual contacts and make room for more deliberate connections. My initial days of social isolation in Minnesota ended naturally once classes started, but it was chance that brought me one of the best opportunities for connecting I could have hoped to find. I was chatting with a couple of colleagues from a different department when one of them said she was teaching an evening course that semester and was hoping that the other colleague would be interested in having dinner with her each week before class. That colleague was too busy, but I eagerly agreed. Those weekly dinners led to a valued friendship, and they taught me more about the institution than I thought possible.

How to Avoid Social Isolation

- Get to know your colleagues, including the staff.
- Don't use introversion or shyness or busyness as an excuse to keep to yourself; connecting in your department is part of the job.
- Build work relationships into your daily schedule by asking colleagues for coffee or lunch or a walk.
- Be on the lookout for allies and potential mentors.
- Be aware of department politics when making friends; be friendly with everyone until you know the lay of the land.
- Maintain and develop professional networks.
- Remember that making social connections with your colleagues is one of the most important things you can do for your future.

Want to learn more? I recommend the following:

Brown, Austin Channing. *I'm Still Here: Black Dignity in a World Made for Whiteness.*
Cain, Susan. *Quiet: The Power of Introverts in a World That Can't Stop Talking.*
Nelson, Trisalyn, and Jessica Early. "How to Counter the Isolation of Academic Life."
Pitcher, Erich. *Being and Becoming Professionally Other: Identities, Voices, and Experiences of U.S. Trans* Academics.*
Russo, Richard. *Straight Man.*

PRINCIPLE 3

———

Build a Team of Mentors

THIS CHAPTER WAS CHALLENGING for me to write because, even though I have had generous mentors from time to time and have done a great deal of mentoring myself, I have never had a formal mentor or consistent mentoring support. I only recently realized what I wasn't getting and how much not getting it mattered. I have had many wonderful women and men who encouraged me and provided guidance and resources that helped me succeed. They provided me great support, but I never got anything like the mentoring I see my white male colleagues receive.

In high school, I didn't have help applying for or selecting a college, and once in college no one suggested that I write an honors thesis or go to graduate school. My adviser was surprised when I successfully did both. None of the faculty who agreed to write letters of recommendation for me actually did so. Meanwhile, I watched one of my white male friends being groomed to become a professor. As an undergraduate, he was on department committees and went to movies with faculty members. Professors bragged about him and speculated about his future accomplishments. In graduate school no one encouraged me to attend conferences or make connections that would allow me to review books or sit on committees or associations in my field. Only once was I encouraged to revise a paper for submission to a journal. No one guided me in how to write a dissertation suitable for revision into a book.

Today I watch my white male colleagues continue to receive assistance from powerful mentors. In just the last couple of years, one of my white male friends, a full professor, has had his dissertation director recommend him for a prestigious position and suggest he revise a graduate school paper for publication. It has been easy to view myself as less deserving of help and attention than my white male friends, but I'm not so sure about that now. Instead, I am convinced that regardless of whether I was deserving, I should have gotten just as much support. That's why it is essential that we mentor women—especially BIPOC and nonbinary women—and that women seek out mentors. Women shouldn't have to struggle so hard. We should be able to put all our energy toward thriving, but we need allies to do that—even if we have to find them ourselves.

Recruiting women and BIPOC men is difficult enough for institutions of higher learning, so once they've been hired, we should do everything possible to retain their much-needed talent. Mentoring is a major element in retention and a crucial part of institutional service that should be recognized as such. As my colleague W. Brad Johnson wrote, however, in *On Being a Mentor: A Guide for Higher Education Faculty*, "although men and women report mentoring that is equivalent in prevalence, women face more barriers to securing a mentorship" (175). While departments that assign mentors to new faculty members likely do so evenhandedly, I suspect that many women don't even know that they're not getting the informal mentoring that men receive.

Johnson points to a study by Lauri Hyers and colleagues that showed no difference in the number of mentoring encounters for white men and BIPOC men, but the difference between all men and all women was discouraging. Men reported nearly one more additional mentoring interaction a week than women did (177). The disparity is invisible. Talking about this with my writing partner, Irene,

I said, "You don't know what you're not getting. You can't see what is not there." She replied, "You don't ask for what you don't know about." This was largely true for both of us. With a few memorable exceptions, we had figured things out on our own, and now we figure things out together. We started as writing partners and have since mentored each other for the past nine years. We have developed a model of horizontal mentoring I think more of us could use.

The traditional definition of a mentor in higher education is a senior member of the department who offers guidance to new faculty based on personal and professional experience. Such vertical mentoring can be a mixed blessing. One of my Latina colleagues views this setup as a very American concept. She described many instances in which she received guidance from senior colleagues, but, she said, there was no concept of "mentoring." Another Latina colleague was especially surprised by my suggestion that we think about mentoring in a less formal way, because she thought of mentors as authority figures. I suggest that mentoring can occur as part of any relationship you have with a colleague, not only one senior to you; it can be anyone you talk to about teaching, scholarship, or service. I want you to think of yourself as a mentor in your professional relationships and for us to think about constantly being in a mutual mentoring relationship with one another.

In responding to a draft of this chapter, my colleague Jason Shaffer, a white man who has benefited from mentoring throughout his career, wrote, "Horizontal, mutual mentoring is the best way to help break the old boys' club model, which invariably only benefits White men." My neighbor Mary Alice Ross said that thinking about mentoring as a more informal structure made her appreciate that she has more mentors than she realized. She wrote in an email, "Mentoring seemed to me like a very formal, rather intimidating process . . . [but] you make it seem much more relaxed and natural." It should be relaxed and natural, so much so that it happens every day.

We all need a team of mutual mentors. You don't have to call them mentors, and you don't have to schedule formal meetings. Five minutes in the hall or at the copier can be a valuable micro-mentoring session.

Remember the story I told at the end of the last chapter about having a weekly dinner with a senior colleague? Neither of us would have described ours as a mentoring relationship, but it was. You should have colleagues you turn to for conversations about teaching; others with whom you share scholarship. You really need people to help with the job market, and still others to guide you in navigating the workplace and its service obligations. Mentors who will help you manage departmental pressure to socialize (or exclusion from socializing) are essential, especially if you are BIPOC, LGBTQ+, nonbinary, or single.

I was discussing with another single woman friend how we felt socially isolated in our departments. I said, "Single women don't get invited to things." "Is that it?" she said, slamming her hand on the table. "I thought it was because I'm Black." I'm also reminded of the time I had a dinner party to introduce a newly hired woman to colleagues from across campus. Her department chair canceled at the last minute because his wife was ill, and he didn't think it appropriate for him to go to a single woman's house by himself. "Well," I said lamely, "my mother will be here." He still didn't come. You need allies to help you manage awkward social interactions. You might find all the support you need in one person, but even if you do, be deliberate about creating circles of colleagues you can trust. You might be assigned an official mentor, who may or may not actually become a mentor to you. Make good use of the relationship, but also find people you can rely on inside and outside of your department as well as outside your institution.

If you're assigned a senior colleague in your department as a formal mentor, don't expect that person to give you everything you need. In fact, it might feel counterproductive. Here are some of the negative experiences that women have shared with me about formal mentoring relationships:

- The power differential can create obstacles to creating a trusting relationship.
- Senior faculty can be intimidating and judgmental or intimidated and competitive.

- Senior men are not always comfortable mentoring women. Cultural differences can make communication difficult; this was especially difficult for BIPOC women assigned to be mentored by older white men possibly harboring debilitating gendered racism.
- Senior female mentors might be inclined to share horror stories that are no longer relevant; don't even ask what "maternity leave" was like back in the day.

It is wise to be cautious when beginning a formal mentoring relationship. It may well develop into a fruitful relationship if your mentor is generous and not jaded by professional disappointment. Even if the pairing is not ideal, you might get a wealth of information at the price of the emotional labor required to shake off the condescension that comes along with your mentor's advice. There are things you need from senior faculty that you can't get from peer mentors, who might not know the history of the department and institution any better than you do. Even if you don't feel you're getting what you need from such a mentor, having the goodwill of someone senior in the department can indirectly support your success.

If you have a formal, assigned mentor, it is likely to be a white man because white males are the majority at the senior level. It's, however, important to have a diverse group of mentors with different institutional perspectives. In response to this chapter, a junior colleague wrote the following reflection about the value of having women mentors:

One thing I was thinking about as I read the draft of this chapter is the gender of mentors. Aside from my dissertation director, who was a man, almost all of my mentors have been women. The horizontal relationships I form are largely pairs or groups of women. And I've seen, at least within my field, that women are more likely to form mentorship communities. I suspect this is in part a response to the old boys' club of academia, but I think it's also in part that forming and sustaining communities involves emotional labor, which women are much more used to being tasked with (and dare I say, better at?). During coronavirus, for example, I've become part of a women's writing Zoom group and a different accountability group organized by the journal *ABO: Women in the Arts*.

Women are invested in mentoring and supporting each other. Also, as a young woman, I have sometimes felt that some (obviously not all) men can be reticent to mentor me, lest the mentorship relationship be perceived the wrong way. I wonder whether that fear has been amplified by #metoo? In any case, it is a loss to women when senior male colleagues shy away from developing informal mentorship relationships with them.

I love the idea of "mentoring communities." I think we are likely a part of such a group without recognizing it as such. Like my junior colleague, many women have shared with me their frustration at being left out of the department's weekly poker game or pickup basketball games or racket ball ladders. Many women don't even realize that these opportunities for informal mentoring are occurring. I once joked that yoga was the new golf. I know many women who have mutual mentoring relationships with their workout partners. As with mentoring communities, we could benefit even more from these relationships if we recognize their inherent professional value, cultivate allies, and practice horizontal micro-mentoring with peers.

While many departments assign mentors to new tenure-track faculty, if you're an adjunct, you will likely need to find your own mentors—but so should we all. Mutual mentoring relationships result from the connections with colleagues that I urged you to develop in the previous chapter. Once you have established connections, you should be able to tell which of your colleagues you can turn to when you need to think through issues ranging from developing a syllabus to writing your annual performance review or tenure package. It rarely works to ask someone to be your mentor because most of us don't know what it would mean to do that. Instead, ask for help with specific things. Remember, it is not a sign of weakness to ask for advice. It is tempting to reject help when it's offered to appear self-sufficient, especially if you're feeling impostor threat, but that would be a mistake. Don't reject a potential mentoring relationship to prove you don't need it. Here are some things you can ask colleagues to do for you—or better yet for each other:

- Review syllabuses and course material.
- Share ideas for what to do on the first day of class and how to learn student names.
- Talk about how to make use of small groups and how to get a discussion going.
- Visit each other's classes; the first time you have a class visit should not be for an evaluation.
- Interpret student evaluations.
- Read each other's CVs, teaching philosophies, and teaching portfolios.
- Discuss grants and conference proposals.
- Exchange research, especially early drafts.
- Consider institutional and departmental policies and unwritten assumptions.
- Get advice about how much service is expected and which service assignments are most burdensome or rewarding.

If you ask a colleague for one of these things, you are more likely to get what you need from the relationship.

Once you have some shared experiences, be sure to appreciate your colleagues' willingness to help you succeed. I have found that saying "Thank you for being such a great mentor to me" is a terrific way to ensure that colleagues will feel invested in your future. Eventually you can get to a place of comfort that will allow you to send an email like "Can we meet for coffee sometime this week? I need some mentoring." I actually got an email like that the other day. How could I say no?

There are plenty of books on how to mentor, but there isn't much advice on how to be mentored. Looking back, I realize that one of the reasons I didn't receive good mentoring was that I had no idea how to get a mentor or, more importantly, how to be mentored. In hindsight, I realize this was what my white male colleagues were learning how to do. They were being coached to expect support and to ask for it when they didn't get it. They were also being trained in how to take advice. If you have selected or been assigned a mentor, and regardless of whether you perceive there to be a true mentoring relationship, you should be prepared to make the most out of your contact with your colleagues and to nurture relationships with them. There is much to criticize about Sheryl Sandberg's *Lean In*, which appears to address only highly privileged women, but her chapter on mentoring (64–76) is one of the best I've read on the subject. It showed me that I didn't know how to be mentored. Sandberg's advice is to educate yourself about the person you wish to be mentored by and have a clear purpose in creating the relationship: Do you want support for your research? Help with your teaching? A guide to institutional culture? Be prepared for meetings with your mentor.

First, to learn about the person mentoring you, read up on some of his or her research. Ask to look at a syllabus. Ask about his or her experience in the department—for all you know he or she was once department chair—and at previous institutions and in graduate school. What was the topic of his or her dissertation? In other words, take the lead in establishing contact and setting an agenda for the relationship. You can be gentle about this, but don't wait for the other person to approach you. Even with an officially assigned mentor, you will do well to suggest meetings beyond the usual initial lunch. Make it a point to check in, however briefly, once a week. You shouldn't have to take the initiative, but chances are you will need to do just that.

Be sure to show gratitude to your mentor. Saying thank you is only the start. Nominate your mentor for committees and awards. Agree to professional requests. This holds true for the mentors you make at your institution and through professional organizations as well as for those you continue to maintain relationships with from graduate school.

Don't limit your field of mentors to the people you happen to run into. Seek out mentors through writing and research groups, even if it means starting one of your own. There are also wonderful programs like HERS (Higher Education Resource Services) that deliberately cultivate mentors for their participants. HERS: Women Leaders in Higher

Education is dedicated to empowering women to seek leadership roles in the field through the HERS Leadership Institute: Higher Education Leadership Development Program. More women in leadership roles is something we desperately need.

I was lucky to have a wonderful mentor in Linda Bennett, then provost and later president of the University of Southern Indiana, where I started a teaching and learning center. I had been teaching for 20 years, but I still needed mentoring as I moved into administrative positions. I would never have considered becoming a dean if Linda hadn't sent me to visit HERS. In early 2022, the institute was operating virtually because of COVID-19, but my experience of it was two and a half glorious weeks at Bryn Mawr under the direction of the now retired, but still amazing, Judith White. We heard panels of female presidents and chief financial officers, we worked on career plans and met with mentors. Most importantly, I made connections with other women developing leadership skills and experiences. I still rely on the amazing group of women I met there, many of whom have gone on to presidencies.

There are other workshops and institutes that will pair you with mentors to support you throughout your career. They require a significant investment in time and money, but participants rarely regret making an investment in themselves. If you can't find institutional funding, many programs offer scholarships. Whenever you participate in an external event, but sure to keep an eye out for potential mentors with whom you can build a relationship. Remember that the other people there are looking for connections too.

The mutual mentoring that I advocate requires mentors to think about what it means to mentor. Being a good mentor is a lot like being a good mentee. The first step is to build a trusting relationship. Do that by actively listening to your mentee to learn as much about them as you can. Active listening is a skill we all need to cultivate and practice. Most of these behaviors come naturally—when we are really listening, instead of planning what to say next. Pay attention to body language; leaning forward and nodding your head are two ways to show you are listening. Ask open-ended (rather than yes or no) questions like "Tell me more about your classes." Ask for clarification and repeat back what your mentee says to ensure that you've understood it correctly: "It sounds to me like you are frustrated by the lack of participation you are getting from your students. Is that the way to describe it?" Be sure to pay attention to emotions that arise during the conversation: Is there a topic that makes your mentee especially anxious? Is there something about which she is especially enthusiastic? These are important things to follow up on. (Take a look at "Workshops" for an overview and an exercise designed to cultivate active listening skills.)

Plan to spend ten or fifteen minutes with your mentee every week in micro-mentoring sessions. You will be amazed at how quickly you can develop a relationship with such a small time commitment if you do it regularly. In these brief meetings, all you really need to do is check in to see how things are going:

- Show interest and concern by asking your mentee about him or herself: background, family, pets, travel, hobbies. Try to find something you have in common.
- Instead of asking "Do you have any questions I can answer?" say "I know you must have lots of questions; maybe I can help answer some of them."
- Be willing to share your experiences—especially examples of feeling like an impostor. It's hard to ask someone if they have impostor syndrome, but you can say "When I first got here, I was worried everyone would find out I was a fraud."
- Maintain confidentiality and be sensitive to the power imbalance inherent in the relationship.
- Share your experiences rather than offering advice, unless you are directly asked for it. Even when someone asks me for advice, I try to come up with a similar situation as an example of something that worked or perhaps didn't.
- Offer to read research, sit in on class, look at annual review and promotion materials.
- Learn from your mentee.

In most formal mentoring programs that I know of, when new faculty are assigned a mentor, they meet for lunch the first semester; this is frequently the end of it. Worse, the lunch usually involves the mentor imparting all their knowledge to the mentee, who gets buried in a landslide of anecdotes—or even worse, diatribes against the administration. That's not mentoring in my book; it's lecturing. In *Advice for New Faculty Members*, Robert Boice describes a model for mentoring that follows his model of brief daily sessions recommended for sustaining research (237–48). In his mentoring model, the mentor and mentee meet for, say, 10 minutes or so, every week (or better, every few days); they continue to do so for two or more years. This allows the pair to build a lasting and meaningful relationship. One of the mentors in Boice's study described the mutual benefits of the program: "I had never been totally clear about what I did as a teacher . . . That took some thinking and observation . . . Then, of course, I put those somewhat clearer techniques to work in my *own* teaching. Now *that* was an unexpected benefit of mentoring. I may be getting more out of this than she [the mentee] is" (245; emphasis in original).

When a mentoring relationship is working well, it can begin to include coaching someone through any number of thorny issues. This is where you need to be especially careful not to give advice unless your mentee asks for it directly. It would be best to spend most of the discussion exploring the situation. What you are striving for as a coach is to help your mentee find her own solution. Asking questions instead of supplying answers is the best way to guide your mentee toward discovering a way through the problem. You can be most helpful by setting goals with your mentee for the next steps and being there for regular progress checks.

I highly recommend going to a coaching workshop, such as Coaching for Greater Effectiveness, run by the Center for Creative Leadership. I was amazed at how much I learned from it, in large part because I received such excellent coaching while there. Part of the workshop involved practicing to coach one another. I presented what I thought was an intractable problem, and by exploring it with the other coaches, I began to see it in an entirely new way. At the workshop,

I learned to use the 5 Stages of Coaching, adapted from Johan Naudé and Florence Plessier's *Becoming a Leader-Coach*:

1. Build a relationship.
2. Learn the details of the situation; be sure to use active listening.
3. Ask questions that will get your mentee to question their assumptions about the situation.
4. Offer support and help identify other sources of support.
5. Set goals for resolving the issue, with dates for completion.

When I'm coaching someone, I have a tendency to jump to solutions too quickly. After I learned to spend more time exploring the problem at hand, I found that the person relaying the situation would arrive at their own solution, which is a much more effective outcome. They often come to conclusions I would have never considered, and they are much more likely to implement their own ideas. It's understandable to want to be the superhero who swoops in and fixes everything, but it's even better to help someone become their own superhero.

I had only been at the Naval Academy for a few weeks when my colleague Rich O'Brien, associate dean of the engineering school, came to me with a problem. Engineering was committed to hiring more women, but they tended not to stay. How, Rich asked, could the academy improve the experience of the women we had worked so hard to recruit? Having departments assign mentors to new faculty members didn't seem to be enough. Rich had also been meeting with new faculty as a group for the first two years, but what could be done beyond that? As we explored the problem, it turned out that Rich already had an idea: more mentoring. But how?

We ultimately decided to bolster departmental efforts with a division-wide mentoring program modeled on Boice's plan of having mentoring pairs meet weekly for 10 to 15 minutes. Faculty members in their third year were invited to participate as mentees. The program the included all new faculty, not just women, because one thing I've learned from teaching is that when I alter an assignment to make it more inclusive, it's good for everyone. We matched each member with a senior faculty volunteer from outside their home departments, and in some cases outside the division.

Rich developed a questionnaire that asked the mentees what area they wanted to concentrate on and asked the mentors in what area they felt best able to provide support. We also inquired about personal interests. We were deliberate in matching people based on a desire to focus on teaching or research, but we found the personal interests were even more helpful in creating a quick rapport between the pairs. For example, we matched bike riders with one another and new parents with folks who had slightly older children. We trained the mentors in mentoring and coaching. The pairs signed an agreement that obligated them to meet regularly but also included a "no fault divorce" clause that allowed either of them to dissolve the partnership for any reason. We then used Planning a Realistic Summer Break—an exercise you can find in "Workshops"—to help them set short-term and long-term goals.

We also set up a system for new faculty to receive regular classroom observations with constructive feedback. This system is based on the model developed by Rebecca Brent and Richard Felder called paired peer observations. It is a fabulous system that provides strong, objective evidence of teaching effectiveness that can be used to counterbalance the subjective responses in student evaluations, which are often marred by unconscious bias against women, particularly BIPOC women. (We will come back to the problem of student evaluations in Principle 6.) Two faculty members, one from within and one from outside the department, talk to the faculty member being observed about the learning objectives for the course, and then they visit the class together. They each fill out an observation checklist designed and tested by Brent and Felder. Afterwards, they work together to complete a single, combined checklist of their observations to present to the observed faculty member.

We have been scheduling observations during faculty members' third year. Prior to going up for tenure, they are again observed, this time twice during the school year. The first visit, early in the semester, is purely formative, with feedback going only to the observed faculty member. The observations from the second visit go to the faculty member as well, but also to the department chair to inform the tenure recommendation. So far, we have had a 100 percent success rate in retaining and tenuring faculty who have participated in the mentoring program. It is a real testimony to the power of mentoring to help faculty succeed and to stay. If your institution doesn't have a mentoring program, or even if it does, create one for yourself, and build a team of mentors to help you and your colleagues thrive.

Finally, pay it forward by being a good mentor to your undergraduate and graduate students and your advisees. Think of yourself as a mentor to all of them—not just the "best" ones whom you want to encourage to follow your footsteps into academic careers. All of our students deserve to be encouraged and nurtured as well as challenged and educated. Some of them will have regularly received mentoring and will know how to seek it out. Others, especially first-generation college students, will need to be taught how to be mentored. As we know, teaching something is the best way to learn it, so think of this as a great way to hone your own skills in being mentored. Look for opportunities to lift up all women and BIPOC men. This is especially important in STEM fields, which are sadly still chilly environments for people who are not white men. We need to diversify talent in STEM, and mentoring is a powerful way to contribute to the pipeline we keep hoping to see develop.

Thriving is more than just succeeding. Thriving is succeeding with joy. Surrounding yourself with colleagues who have a vested interest in your success brings joy and compassion to your work relationships. Professional companionship is a natural extension of your connections with colleagues. It takes time to nurture these relationships, but it will create the intellectual community we went into academia to find.

How to Be Mentored and Be a Mentor

- Take the initiative.
- Educate yourself about potential mentors.
- Develop mutual mentoring relationships with peers.

- Build a team of mentors.
- Engage in regular micro-mentoring sessions.
- Nurture mentoring relationships with regular check-ins and gratitude.
- Coach with careful listening to help the other person discover her own solution.
- Mentor your students and teach them how to be mentored.

Want to learn more? I recommend the following:

Brent, Rebecca, and Richard Felder. "A Protocol for Peer Review of Teaching."

HERS (Higher Education Resource Services): Women Leaders in Higher Education, www.hersnetwork.org.

Johnson, W. Brad. *On Being a Mentor: A Guide for Higher Education Faculty.*

Naudé, Johan, and Florence Plessier. *Becoming a Leader-Coach: A Step-by-Step Guide to Developing Your People.*

PRINCIPLE 4

———

Manage Your Time

I KNEW I WAS IN TROUBLE when I asked my older daughter, then age 5, what she wanted to get her father for his birthday. Pippa responded, "I'll call a meeting with Sadie [her 2-year-old sister] and get back to you."

Before I had children, I didn't think about work-life balance. One of the things I valued about being an academic was the way my work integrated with my life. I would do prep reading in bed and write all weekend. I once spent an entire Thanksgiving break creating notes on Restoration drama for the rest of the semester. I vividly remember the day I was so deep in thought about teaching John Donne that after I dropped Sadie at daycare, I drove to work with Pippa still in her car seat. After I parked, I was startled by the tiny voice from the backseat that said, "Don't I have to go to school today?"

I don't regret working so much, but I do regret that even when I was spending time with my family, I was still thinking about work instead of fully enjoying our time together. Women still typically take on more housework and childcare than their male partners. Even though the (heteronormative) data that Alice Eagly and Linda Carli present in *Through the Labyrinth: The Truth about How Women Become Leaders* is from the early 2000s, it sadly still rings true: time diary studies in which couples recorded hours spent doing housework and childcare showed that women spent 19 hours a week doing housework, while men contributed 11, and that women did more than double the amount of childcare than men. Altogether, women spent 3.8 hours on housework and childcare for every hour that men put in (50-51). In addition, Eagly and Carli point out, "Married women do more housework than single women" (51). If you hadn't lived with a man at that time, surely you would've had compassion for those who did. They note that attitudes about childcare had changed—putting pressure on women that resulted in their spending more time on it than previous generations, whereas "changes in attitudes about fathers' childcare responsibilities have outpaced changes in behavior" (52). In other words, it sucked.

That was some 20 years ago, but if you're feeling overwhelmed today, you still have good reason; you are also not alone. I can tell you, however, that if you have small children, it will get better—at least in terms of time commitment; the emotional stress, though, might get worse. I don't have a solution for the tug of war caused by the demands of family and work, but I know what I didn't do to make it better: I didn't plan. I didn't manage my time. I didn't work efficiently. I didn't stop working at the end of the workday, which is especially challenging when working from home. I wish I had found Boice's brief daily sessions earlier (41-46, 139-43) to help me get things done without wearing myself out (as discussed in Principle 7, Make Scholarship a Habit). Boice's strategy is just what it says it is, and it applies to everything. Lately I have been practicing what I call "incremental gardening." I used to wait until I had a free weekend afternoon to work in the yard until my back and legs were so sore I could hardly stand up the next day. By the time I'd recovered and found another block of time, I was right back where I had started. Now I limit myself to forty-five minutes of gardening in the early evening. I'm enjoying the garden more and can see the progress made every day. Boice describes his strategy in detail as it applies to teaching and research, but it works for any big project.

One of my biggest regrets about the way I failed to manage my time is that I rarely gave myself time off. There are plenty of books and articles on how women still spend a disproportionate amount of time on childcare and domestic duties. As a single parent of two children, that was certainly my experience. Thankfully, there are more accommodations for children than when mine were young—for example, parental leave didn't exist back then—but the struggles I see my colleagues going through make it clear that academia is still not doing enough to nurture women faculty—especially women with children. When more of us are in positions of power, I hope we will change that.

I realize that each of the principles in this book adds yet another item to the list of things for you to do, but each of them pays off by setting you up for a thriving career. Don't forget: time spent planning will save you time in the end. Today there are tons of self-help books on time management, but the first big one was Steven Covey's *7 Habits of Highly Effective People*. What has stayed with me from this classic is his advice about setting priorities and ignoring the little time-consuming things that tend to drive our days. Covey has a famous exercise in which he asks a seminar participant to fit a pile of rocks, stones, and pebbles and a bucket of sand into a box; there are YouTube videos of it if you want to see it in action. The participant's instinct was to try to get as much as possible into the box by first pouring in the sand, then putting the stones and pebbles in, and leaving the big rocks for last. Of course, this didn't work. If you start with the big rocks, however, the stones and pebbles get nestled in, and the sand poured over them fills in the gaps. In my office we set priorities by asking each other what our big rocks are. That's where we need to start the day. My big work rock is always research. For me, teaching—which includes faculty development workshops as well as regular academic courses—represents the stones and pebbles. Email is the sand.

Your calendar, not your email, should set your priorities for the day. It's hard to do, but try to check your email at the top of the hour instead of as it appears in your inbox. The same is true with texts and social media. Otherwise, it can all be a bottomless time sink. I have a note in my syllabus that explains that I check my email regularly from 8:00 to 4:00, Monday through Friday, but only occasionally on evenings and weekends. If you manage your students' expectations, they will understand (and because I do check email on evenings and weekends, when I respond to them, they are grateful instead of impatient). My colleague Samara Firebaugh recommends keeping your work emails and personal emails in separate accounts so that when you check in with your mother in the evening, you aren't swept back into work by accident. Also, be thoughtful about your emails and texts to others. Don't send a text to the dean at 2:00 in the morning about an advisee you're worried about. Don't send an urgent request to colleagues at 4:30 on a Friday afternoon. Realize that your priorities are not the same as everyone else's, and don't let other people's priorities drive your day.

The above brings us to Covey's elegant and useful four quadrants ("Habit 3: Put First Things First"):

Quadrant 1—Urgent and important
Quadrant 2—Not urgent but important
Quadrant 3—Urgent but not important
Quadrant 4—Neither urgent nor important (167–212)

You need to take care of things in quadrant 1, but you should strive to keep this quadrant as empty as possible. This can be challenging if you have children or are an administrator. Quadrant 2 is where you should aim to spend most of your time, in part to prevent things from moving into quadrant 1. Keep your research and teaching preparation in quadrant 2. I think one of the most important things to keep in quadrant 2 is planning your day, week, month, and year. (For help with that, see Planning a Realistic Summer Break, in "Workshops.") Quadrant 3 is where things that are important to other people reside. Try to stay here as little as possible; design systems that will help you move quickly through the items in this quadrant. For example, create templates for letters of recommendation. Replace lengthy email responses with a phone call. The key here is efficiency. Ignore quadrant 4. Anything there will move to another quadrant or, more likely, go away.

I have found Covey's four quadrants extremely helpful in setting priorities, particularly when I'm feeling overwhelmed. There have been times when I've divided my desk into them and put materials and sticky notes into their rightful quadrants. It's a much better system than the one I often find myself using, which is to ask, "What's the next thing that could cause me public embarrassment?" It's an effective question, but planning ahead is better.

Part of good planning depends on working efficiently when you do have a chance to work. Having children forced me to reckon with this. I didn't have time for inspiration to strike. I had to learn to work in short bits of time. Who knew if nap time would last an hour or 10 minutes? Knowing what I had to do was essential, and I had to get right to it—no dawdling—or I might miss whatever window I had. In "Why Wait? The Science behind Procrastination," Eric Jaffe offers a readable run down of the research on procrastination. Jaffe quotes Joseph Ferrari's useful distinction between procrastinating and procrastinators:

> "What I've found is that while everybody may procrastinate, not everyone is a procrastinator," says APS Fellow Joseph Ferrari, a professor of psychology at DePaul University. He is a pioneer of modern research on the subject, and his work has found that as many as 20 percent of people may be chronic procrastinators.
>
> "It really has nothing to do with time-management," he says. "As I tell people, to tell the chronic procrastinator to *just do it* would be like saying to a clinically depressed person, *cheer up*." (emphasis in Jaffe's original)

Science is still busy trying to figure out what's up with chronic procrastinators, but for the other 80 percent or so of us, it's often a matter of just doing it instead of putting it off for "future me" to take care of. We have a standing joke around the house about all the things "future me" is going to accomplish, like taking out the trash and finishing this chapter. As Jane McGonigal wrote in *Slate*, "FMRI [functional magnetic resonance imaging] studies suggest that when you imagine your future self, your brain does something weird: It stops acting as if you're thinking about yourself. Instead, it starts acting as if you're thinking about *a completely different person*" (emphasis in original). No wonder putting things off feels so good. We have just delegated the task to someone else. I think remembering that "future me" is still "me" holds the key to normal procrastination. In a workshop I did on time management, one of the participants came up with a great idea for dealing with "future me." "From now on," he said, "I'm going to imagine 'future me' as lazy and incompetent. Then I'll think, 'I couldn't possibly leave this up to "future me." Just imagine what a mess he would make of the job.'"

It is easy to confuse procrastination with a lack of focus. Often we just feel too distracted to get anything done. I attended a talk by Carl Steinhorst where he described distraction as "confusion about what matters." I confess that at one point I was so distracted that I had a hard time focusing on this chapter, which is more than a little ironic. I had a meeting with my writing partner, a staff meeting, lots of emails about an upcoming workshop, ideas about a future set of workshops, lots of errands, and texts with a friend who was also having trouble focusing. Argh. I had to resort to cleaning off my desk, which I finds helps me refocus. You likely have your own strategies; the trick is to use them deliberately and mindfully. Steinhorst's *Can I Have Your Attention* is full of ideas to help you focus, among them listening to music without words, doodling, and having meetings while walking. What's going on with these examples is that you are using physical activity—listening, drawing, walking, breathing mindfully—in other words, giving yourself something to do, so that your mind can better focus. Have you ever had an important idea in the shower, while vacuuming, cooking, driving? It's the same principle.

Sometimes we have so many decisions to make that we can't think straight. Once while driving home from a conference, the car broke down. My partner made a series of big, stressful decision about what to do. At dinner, the server asked her what kind of salad dressing she wanted. She just looked at the server, mouth open, completely unable to decide. She had what Roy Baumeister and John Tierney call "decision fatigue" in their fascinating, research-driven book *Willpower: Rediscovering the Greatest Human Strength*.

It turns out, we have a finite amount of willpower, and every decision or act of impulse control uses up some of it. This leads to "ego depletion," which results in diminished willpower, stronger cravings, overreacting and emotional responses, difficulty making decisions, and reduced creativity (88–107). Based on Baumeister's research, it doesn't look like we can increase our willpower, but there are things that can help. In the short term, eat something, especially protein. Making decisions and exercising willpower feel like they take energy, and they actually do. Eating something gives you more calories to burn. I keep raw almonds in my desk drawer for just this purpose. In the long run, it helps to reduce decision making.

All this take us back to the importance of planning. You can take five minutes in the morning to plan your day, but there are lots of other things you can do ahead of time to reduce the number of decisions you have to make at that time, thus saving your energy for the more important things, like what you're going to do in class. Here are a few things you can do the night before, after dinner has refreshed you a bit, but I'm sure you can think of more: pick out your clothes for the next day, decide what to have for breakfast, set up coffee or tea, make your lunch, pack your briefcase. If you have children, get them to do some of these things the night before, too (but good luck with that).

At its worst, ego depletion becomes what Daniel Goleman calls "amygdala hijack." Goleman, who's well known for his work on emotional intelligence, explains amygdala hijack in his book *Focus*: The amygdala is the part of the brain that experiences emotions, and it takes over, or hijacks, our thinking when we experience strong or sudden emotions, especially anger or regret. This happens more easily if we're already experiencing ego depletion. This happened to me recently when after fasting for some blood work, I realized that I had left my ID card at home. Without my ID, I wouldn't be able to get onto campus at the Naval Academy. At that point, not only was I hungry, I also risked being late for an important meeting. I drove back home to pick up my ID only to discover that a terrible accident involving several cars and a bicycle had closed down the road into my neighborhood. The police waved us all back onto the highway. As I merged, panic overcame me. It felt unsafe to drive, but I had no choice. I couldn't think what to do or where to go. My amygdala was in control.

Fortunately, I had just been to a talk by Goleman on this exact problem. Following his advice, I did a breathing exercise he had led at the talk: breathe in for four counts, hold it for one count, breath out for four counts. This exercise is likely familiar, especially if you do yoga, but I don't think I would have thought to use it in this situation, when I was telling myself, "Think! Think! Think!"—which made me realize I couldn't think. It worked like a charm. I calmed down and came up with a solution. I even made it to the meeting on time. The mindfulness exercise helped me regain cognitive control by producing calm. When we are calm, the amygdala is less triggered and recovers faster, making us more resilient.

McGonigal describes a number of ways to increase resiliency in her amazing book *SuperBetter: The Power of Living Gamefully*. She also has a great TED Talk, "The Game That Can Give You 10 Extra Years of Life," during which she leads the audience in activities to increase resiliency and thus live longer and happier lives. This is the ultimate in time management, right? Here's a quick description of the exercise (which you can find in *SuperBetter*, 159–83), but it's more fun to watch the TED Talk and play along:

1. Exercise—even just a walk down the hall or raising your arms over your head for five seconds—to increase physical resiliency.
2. Concentrate on a set task, like snapping your fingers fifty times or counting back from 100 by sevens, to increase intellectual resiliency.
3. Look at pictures of baby animals to increase emotional resiliency.
4. Send a thank you note, write down one thing you are grateful for, or shake hands to increase social resiliency.

McGonigal is a video game designer with a PhD from the University of California, Berkeley. Among other things, she teaches at Stanford. I cite her credentials because it's easy to dismiss her work given that it deliberately involves fun. Women lose credibility easily enough, but especially if we fail to present ourselves with due seriousness. McGonigal's work is research based, but she is deliberately approachable and playful. This is in keeping with her thesis that we should live our lives more "gamefully."

When we play a game, we don't (usually) get as frustrated when we lose as when we're trying to solve a research problem or a challenge at home or in class and find it too difficult and fail. With games, we just play it again. McGonigal argues that we should apply that same gaming mindset to our real world challenges. Coupled with increased resiliency, we will become more creative problem solvers and more balanced in our work and lives. I think that is really what we are all striving to achieve.

There are lots of books out there offering suggestions about how to balance work and the rest of life. I'm sure you have your favorites. I have never found one that seemed like a magic bullet. None of the insights I've shared here can magically solve the problem of the work-life balance. I think that taken all together, they can help us work more efficiently and effectively—and that leaves more time for the other parts of life.

I have learned to manage my time by doing a regular exercise involving long-term and short-term planning that includes setting aside time for friends, family, and myself. I do this before winter, spring, and summer breaks. (You can find the template I created for it in Planning a Realistic Summer Break, in "Workshops.") Long-term planning helps me identify the big rocks for the next five to ten years. Short-term planning allows me to think hard about how much I can realistically accomplish in the next few weeks or months; it also helps me plan for downtime, when I'm not trying to relax in spite of being anxious about what I'm not getting done.

I do this exercise with the new faculty group that meets weekly during the academic year. It is more fun to do it in a group or with a mentor, where you can troubleshoot together and pair up for account-ability check-ins. We inevitably realize that a plan to revise a dissertation, clean out the garage, spend quality time with family and friends, take a couple of trips, and prepare for class isn't realistic. Better to figure that out at the beginning than spend the break anxious and in the end frustrated. My colleague Liliana Velasquez Montoya wrote to me about this planning exercise: "As humans we have multiple facets, and we should include those in our planning. Something that resonated with me a lot about Covey's 7 *Habits* is that we only tend to plan for work. However, when we only plan for our professional selves and leave our other portions for whatever time is left, that's when guilt and imbalances start to bother us. We should be sure to use your planning template for our family, friends, and community as well as our spiritual/explorer/artist selves."

One of the best things about plans is how helpful they are when things go wrong. During one winter break, I got pneumonia and spent most of it in bed. Because I had my plan, I didn't wake up from fevered dreams of failure. Instead, I knew exactly what I wasn't going to accomplish, and I was clear about what I had to accomplish. I jettisoned my research expectations, and when I'd recovered sufficiently, I prepared for classes. A colleague had a similar experience. He had seven children, and over the break they each got stomach flu—one after the other. "I've never done so much laundry," he said in January. "But at least I had a plan I could revise."

If you turned to this chapter first, you're not alone. Tori Johnson, one of the many women who read early chapters of this book, asked me to jump ahead and write it so she could read it immediately. I'm not sure this chapter will tell you anything you don't know already, but I hope it will remind you of ways you have succeeded in managing your time. After Irene Lietz, my longtime writing partner, read a draft of the chapter, she said, "Since I retired, I have completely forgotten to plan." This chapter inspired her to reorganize her white board into Covey's four quadrants. She realized that she had been spending time on things that are neither important nor urgent—because those were the things she liked to do. We ended our weekly phone call by agreeing to go write. Then there's Mary Alice Ross, who lives next door and called me over to the fence to happily inform me that she was exhausted and that it was my fault. "After I read your chapter," she said, "I realized that the most urgent and important thing I had to do was get salt and fill my water filter system." Unfortunately, the salt comes in 40-pound bags.

How to Balance Work and Life

- Manage your time by establishing priorities with long-term and short-term planning. (For a template to help with this, see Planning a Realistic Summer Break, in "Workshops.")
- Prep for classes and do scholarship in brief daily sessions (Boice).
- Practice increasing focus (Steinhorst).
- Recognize when you have decision fatigue and ego depletion (Baumeister and Tierney).
- Address amygdala hijack through mindfulness (Goleman).
- Increase resiliency (McGonigal).

Want to learn more? I recommend the following:

Baumeister, Roy F., and John Tierney. *Willpower: Rediscovering the Greatest Human Strength.*
Boice, Robert. *Advice for New Faculty Members: Nihil Nimus.*
Goleman, Daniel. *Focus: The Hidden Driver of Excellence.*
McGonigal, Jane. *SuperBetter: The Power of Living Gamefully* and "The Game That Can Give You 10 Extra Years of Life."
Steinhorst, Carl, with Jonathan McKee. *Can I Have Your Attention? Inspiring Better Work Habits, Focusing Your Team, and Getting Stuff Done in the Constantly Connected Workplace.*

PRINCIPLE 5

Connect with Your Students

I TAUGHT FIRST-YEAR COMPOSITION throughout graduate school, and for me, it was a political commitment to level the playing field through literacy for my largely first-generation, working-class students. My classes were racially and ethnically diverse, with lots of adult learners going back to college because of layoffs. I found it challenging and rewarding. Because it was so clear to them that they needed to improve their writing and communication skills, teaching them felt effortless.

I was also thrilled that in my first job after getting my PhD at a small liberal arts college in the Midwest, I got to teach literature and critical theory, even though I had eight different preps the first year. I didn't change my teaching style from my grad school days even though the students were nearly all college-aged, middle class, and almost all white. My enthusiasm for the material carried me along. I even taught an entire course on Laurence Sterne's *The Life and Opinions of Tristram Shandy, Gentleman.* I loved it. My students applauded my enthusiasm, but they weren't motivated in the same way as the students I had taught previously. I had not yet realized that different students need different things. I actually wondered if they were learning at all. On top of that, I was exhausted.

Looking back, it is easy to see why I was burning out. The first reason is that I had fallen in love with designing new courses. Even when I repeated teaching a course, I couldn't resist the urge to redesign it. It was just so much fun to reimagine the survey course, the Shakespeare course, the theory course, the fist-year composition course, and then there were new courses, in medieval literature, women's literature, British modernism. For ten years I never stopped creating new courses. In addition, there was the prep: I let course development eat up my summer and winter breaks, and I let course prep eat up my evenings and weekends.

If I could give my former self one piece of advice, it would be to teach the same classes with only minor tweaks and focus more on pedagogy than content. I could have used the time and energy I saved on research. Most people say that it takes three or four times through a new course before they really have a sense of the pacing and of what works well. Instead of making major changes, focus on small changes and making classes more active. (For more on recovering from burnout, see my essay "The Emotional Balancing Act of Teaching: A Burnout Recovery Plan.")

The second reason is an even bigger one: I was trying to be the teacher I had wished I had had. In some respects, this was a good thing. I worked hard to create engaging and interactive lectures and lively discussions. I intentionally posed questions that I couldn't answer so it would make us read closely in class and lead us to insights. I was learning so much from my own classes! They were exactly the sort of classes I had wanted to take as an undergraduate, but the energy required for that kind of teaching was enormous. I felt like I was carrying the class in my arms. Worse yet, I wasn't getting the sorts of papers that I thought my students should be capable of producing.

Eventually, everything I felt led me to a devastating realization: The instructor and classes I had wanted were not the ones my students wanted. It should have been apparent to me that I had not been a typical undergraduate. No faculty member probably was. Most of our students don't aspire to go to graduate school. Most of them, even the English majors, don't even like to read. There it was—I had no idea who these students really were or what they wanted from my class. Now I was burned out as well as depressed.

Fortunately for me, I ended up having a conversation with a colleague in educational philosophy that transformed my thinking about teaching. I was describing an exercise I had done in class that had delighted me. "Oh," she said, "you're a constructivist." I'm a what, now? Apparently, I needed to educate myself about my own teaching style. What I discovered changed me as a teacher and rescued me from burnout: I had embraced critical pedagogy, and as a feminist, I've tried to put what I believe into action by sharing power and giving students agency in designing our classes, but this was more philosophy than pedagogy. Constructivism holds that learners construct their own knowledge; this belief leads to active learning strategies that help students do just that. Once I discovered that I was a constructivist, I realized that my goal shouldn't have been to prepare for myself, but to prepare for the students. It instantly got easier. Figuring out who I am as a teacher helped me understand how to relate to my students. Constructivism is not the only way to do this, but it works for me. (Find out what your teaching philosophy is by taking the 4 STEP Quiz, in "Workshops.")

Constructivism is based on the work of Jean Piaget (1896–1980), the Swiss evolutionary biologist whose theories about how learning works have been subsequently substantiated by neurological studies that inform brain-based learning. Piaget applied the theory of evolution to the brain, hypothesizing that we construct our understanding of the world and keep what works, getting rid of ideas that don't. As we go through life, our mental models evolve to make sense of our experiences. The mental model changes as it gets tested and challenged, becoming increasingly complex. That, for Piaget, is the learning process.

My favorite example of how this process works is a description in "Mental Models of the Earth," by Stella Vosniadou and William

Brewer, involving elementary school children studying our planet. Here's my oversimplified version of this complex study: Pretest: Earth is flat—True, based on the children's lived experience. The teacher challenges this model by providing new information: Earth is round—Everyone aces the test. Then there's another test: Earth is round—True; Earth is flat—True. The students had adjusted their mental models to accommodate their lived experience and the new information to create a vision of the Earth as both round and flat—like a pancake (549). You can't just present them with new information; you must also challenge mental models by engaging students to discover what they already know or believe and then alter those models, in this case, by having them actively interact with a globe, demonstrations, or visuals of Earth as seen from the moon. Once I discovered active learning, I realized that I had been trying to do it all along, but I was making it up as I entered every single class. It's no wonder I was exhausted. I didn't know there was a wheel I was trying to reinvent. Now my students do the work, and therefore the learning as well. I gain knowledge about them by watching them learn. That's how teaching became satisfying and energizing.

Recent research rarely acknowledges Piaget. I suppose it doesn't need to since science now confirms his ideas and supports active learning, but it cheers me to no end that he was right all along. Great places to read about the science of learning are in *How Learning Works: 7 Research-Based Principles for Smart Teaching*, by Susan Ambrose and colleagues, and *Small Teaching: Everyday Lessons from the Science of Learning*, by James Lang. Both books aggregate what we now know about how the brain learns and provide concrete learner-centered, active learning practices that promote student engagement.

Active learning is anything that engages students—discussing, writing, doing, thinking—and the bonus is that it's engaging for faculty too. As my colleague Sommer Gentry said, "Active learning strategies help me avoid burn out because I teach *students*—not calculus. So it's a different class every time." Active learning also promotes our developing relationships with our students. My colleague Silvia Peart urged me to emphasize that point in this chapter, writing, "We teach students, so relationships are far more important than content. As graduate students we are taught that the most important thing is the content, so we spend hours reading and preparing our classes, which is all right, but we forget that we are working with human beings."

Of course, we were drawn to our various disciplines because of the content, and you can "cover" a lot more content in a lecture than through active learning. I love a good lecture, which is primarily what college was for me. When I had a class that began with moving all the desks into a circle, my stomach would drop. If I walked into one of my own classes today, I would turn around and walk out. I hated all the sharing and the activities, but I have to admit, I learn more in situations like that because I created knowledge for myself—as Piaget says we do when we're learning.

When teachers lecture, we are asking students to do rote learning, to in essence memorize everything we say. I can't begin to count the number of times a colleague has said in frustration, "I've told them XYZ a dozen times!" We really do seem to think they'll remember everything we say. Despite this, we know that people remember about half of a lecture right after they hear it and that memory begins to erode immediately. Not only that, none of us—teachers or students— can control which half of what was said gets remembered. Many of my colleagues insist that students just need to take better notes. Even assuming they have the ability to figure out how to do that, reviewing notes is not an effective way to study. It's just rote learning—again.

In *Small Teaching,* Lang explains the plight of the frustrated student who studies for hours and still bombs an exam: "Such a student is laboring under the illusion of fluency, possibly because he engaged in common study strategies like reading the textbook or reviewing his notes over and over again. The literature on human learning repeatedly reveals, however, that those strategies prove effective primarily for short-term learning" (51). What, then, is effective in getting knowledge into long-term memory? If we understand more about how students learn, we can be more empathetic—and therefore more effective—as we guide them to really learn about a subject. First, we need to understand the limits of short-term memory.

Short-term or working memory, is not only time limited, it's also space limited. Short-term memory is finite. There's only so much you can store in it. It works perfectly well if you cram the night before a test, filling your brain with bits and pieces of information, as long as you don't need too much storage space. If you have to draw on complex concepts, which should be stored in your long-term memory but aren't, you might be out of luck. Even more problematic, short-term memory has no organizational structure. I think of it as a gumball machine full of individual factoids. If you're lucky, the right one will drop out when you turn the handle. Long-term memory, on the other hand, will expand to accommodate new learning and do it in an organized manner. I think of it as a university. When disciplines change, we add a new major. If the institution grows, we build a new building or add a new dormitory. (Sadly, this doesn't usually apply to parking.) If we are looking for research material, we know to go to the library. If we have a question about thermodynamics, we go to the Mechanical Engineering Department.

There are sidewalks and roads at the university that lead us to all the places we need to go. These paths are key. In the brain, they are the neural pathways that organize and connect knowledge. We prepare the way for them when we retrieve knowledge from our short-term memories, and we build these connections when we sleep. The more we know about something, the denser the neural pathways around that topic become, and the denser the pathways, the easier it is to add to new information about a subject. This is one of the reasons it's hard to teach novices; they have no pathways connecting the pieces of a new subject, and it is difficult as an expert to remember what it was like not to know the topic.

Lang's *Small Teaching* is a fabulous and practical book on ways to promote effective long-term learning. The chapters are packed with the science of learning and the implications for teaching using techniques like prediction, spaced repetition, and interleaving. Lang is a superb distiller of theory and practice, and his column in the *Chronicle of Higher Education* is a must read. I also recommend Maryellen Weimer's *Learner-Centered Teaching: Five Key Changes to Practice*, which was practically a bible for me when I began to use active learning strategies more deliberately. My students were resistant at first, complaining that I was making them teach the class. Today, students have been doing things like small-group work in high school, so it comes more naturally to them once they get to college, and it likely does for you, too, if you've had experiences with active learning as a student.

I think it's important to keep students on board by explaining why you're doing what you're doing—or better yet, inviting them to figure it out. My favorite question in class is "Why did we do that?" My students usually come up with better answers than I do, and I discover more about how they're learning. I had a first-year composition class that asked that we start our Friday sessions with a video. They picked out some good ones. The class favorite was "Friends Forever," an Android commercial montage of unlikely animal pairs playing together and helping each other out: a dog swims with a dolphin, a baby elephant digs with a goat, and so on, all to the song "Robin Hood and Little John Running through the Forest." It's adorable. Some of the students would sing the song coming into class as a hint that they wanted to watch it, so I thought I would play it a second time. Halfway through, I realized that my decision seemed pretty random. At the end of the video, I asked the class, "Why did I play that for you today?" I had nothing, other than maybe adding a little cheer to the day. Everyone looked puzzled, and then someone said, "Because we are doing peer review today, and you wanted to remind us to work together." Brilliant. I think that probably was my unconscious motive. Being transparent about your pedagogical choices increases student buy in, promotes their engagement, and thus improves their learning. It also mitigates the risk of trying something new, because by sharing the reasons, you invite them to join you in the educational process. Now you're all in it together. You're teaching human beings as well as content.

In *Geeky Pedagogy*, a fun-to-read book with an awesome bibliography, Jessamyn Neuhaus makes the crucial point that who we are, and who our students are, impacts our classes before they even begin:

Our race, gender expression, age, ethnicity, economic class, physical appearance and abilities, sexual orientation, and speaking voice all affect how students perceive us, how they accept our authority and our expertise, and how they respond to different pedagogical approaches we might implement. Women teach in a different context than men, and professors of color teach in a different context than white professors, and anything they do in their pedagogical approaches and interactions with students will have a different impact on learning and teaching than it does for white, cisgendered male professors. (24)

If we engage with our students as individuals, recognizing their intersectional identities, as active learning ideally promotes, then we honor the different contexts within which each student is learning. This is why learning that I was a constructivist helped me discover that different students need different things. It is my experience that active learning is as effective for my BIPOC students as for my white students, women and men, LGBTQ+, and straight students. It is also effective for the faculty and professionals outside the academy who've attended my workshops. Nevertheless, it is important to continue to advocate for more research on faculty and student identities and the effectiveness of active learning.

In "Good Teachers Know That Bodies Matter," Koritha Mitchell writes a review of William Germano and Kit Nicholls's *Syllabus: The Remarkable, Unremarkable Document That Changes Everything* and explains why she strives to establish community on the first day of class by recognizing students' identities: "Being a Black woman has meant having my authority challenged in ways that my White colleagues— whether male or not—seldom encounter. But being read as straight, as cisgender, as normatively able has also yielded a level of acceptance of my rightful presence, which must be understood if I am going to be what I am trying to inspire my students to be: lifelong learners."

It has certainly been my experience that students make judgments and assumptions about me before I even open my mouth. I don't look like the authority figure many of them imagine a college professor to be. Aging has done wonders for my authority in the classroom, but

I know that this hasn't been the case for my BIPOC colleagues, who face student doubt about their qualifications. Please, if you are white, use that unearned privilege to raise up your BIPOC colleagues by telling your students about their accomplishments and praising their credentials. I have heard white men say that BIPOC women should tell students how qualified they are to be professors. I'm sure this would work just fine for the white men, but I know this wouldn't work for me. I imagine the students rolling their eyes and writing about my arrogance in their evaluations. So to repeat, if you've been granted authority, use it to support your colleagues who should have it as well but are too often "presumed incompetent"—which is the title of an extraordinary couple of books of essays on class, race, and gender in higher education edited by Yolanda Flores Niemann, Gabriella Gutiérrez y Muhs, and Carmen G. González.

I frequently have moments when I think Would this have happened if I were a white man? I usually suspect that it would not. A student recently emailed me, outraged about his grade for an essay: "I was just a little frustrated and confused with how I received such a low grade on paper number 2. I spent a lot of time and knew that it was worth 20% and then received a C which I was confused with. A C for this paper will hurt my overall grade." The subtext was clear: Who are YOU to give ME a C?!?! It was a challenge to my authority dripping with white male privilege. How do I respond to such verbal assaults? What works for me is to pretend to ignore the implied challenge. In this case, I wrote back, "I know, right? I was so disappointed for you." When I checked in with him before the next class, it turned out that he hadn't been reading my comments on his papers, which explains why I had been writing the same thing over and over all semester.

To be fair, I also get this sort of fury from white female students. In contrast, my BIPOC students tend to stay after class and quietly ask, "Can I talk to you about my paper?" You bet they can, and that's what my insubordinate student ultimately asked because I kept checking on him despite the toxic haze wafting around him. At the end of our paper conference, I asked him what helped him most in class. "When we go through the poem line by line," he said. "Maybe we could do that first before talking about it in small groups?" "That's a great idea," I replied. "Let's do that in the next class, and I'll be sure to give you credit for the suggestion." He beamed at me all the way through our Zoom chat. At our next class, when we did what he had suggested and I acknowledged that it had been his idea, he lit up again.

I still get pushback from students when I correct them. This semester I had to defend myself when students misread poems and insisted that it was my opinion versus theirs. This came up in my Formative Analysis of Classroom Teaching (FACT), our Center for Teaching and Learning's incredibly effective program for getting anonymous, mid-semester feedback from students. For a question about something that hinders students' learning, I got two similarly worded responses along the lines of "My interpretation of the poem compared to professor's; seems as if there is only one correct interpretation of the poems." Argh! What to do? (See "Workshops" for a description of the process that we at the Naval Academy call FACT, the best acronym I've ever created: Don't guess what's working in class, use FACTs).

As I thought about the students' comments, I realized that they really didn't understand that not everything about a poem is subjective. I decided to give them past examples of misreadings, as opposed to interpretations. At first, I was irritated that I even needed to do this, but as I rounded up the examples, I realized that they truly didn't understand that I was correcting them to prevent them from failing. By the time I got to class, I wasn't feeling defensive anymore. I asked the students, "What would have happened on the exam if I hadn't corrected the misreadings?" That seemed to resonate. Next semester, I'm going to explain this up front. Although I don't think I would have gotten pushback if I had been a man, it became clear to me that the distinction between understanding what a poem is saying and interpreting it is something that I needed to make overt. Understanding the difference would help students become better readers. What began as an annoyance thus became a gift.

It doesn't usually feel like a gift to wonder if I'm being treated differently because I'm a woman. It's irritating and exhausting. While I might be challenged more frequently because students think that everything in English class is subjective, I have heard plenty of similar stories from women teaching in STEM. Students expect more partial credit because it's assumed they will be nicer. One colleague recounted a story in which a student flatly told her "You're wrong," after she had explained a theorem. It is important—although it requires even more emotional work, which I resent—not to take your annoyance out on the students when they say such things. They are uneducated. It is our job to teach them to know better, and I think we do that in part just by having the positions we hold and being adults about it. They may treat us as though we don't have authority, but they are wrong. At the end of the day, we give out the grades.

It helps to treat what feels like a challenge to our authority as if the intent were innocent. My wonderful group of readers pointed out that men give awful advice about how to handle such things, because they don't understand that what works for them will not always work for us. Sometimes women need to handle things differently, and in the end it gets better results, even though it puts us in an uncomfortable position. It's good for students to see different leadership styles. When they throw zingers at us in student evaluations, and they will, we need to address this by explaining the context and educating those who'll be reading the evaluations. I know—that's yet another burden—but there are lots of resources to help with this. (We will talk more about this fraught subject in the next principle, "Reflect on Teaching and Student Evaluations.") Maybe the best way to sum it all up is this: Don't be intimidated by your students. Building a relationship with them from the start will prevent a lot of stressful situations and earn you some grace. Students will forgive almost anything if they think you care about their learning.

Neuhaus is rightfully critical of the scholarship of teaching and learning for not taking identity into consideration. Not everything will work for every instructor, and not everything will work for every group of students. Claude Steele's work on stereotype threat taught us this. Steele describes stereotype threat as "whenever we're in a situation where a bad stereotype about one of our own identities could be applied to us—such as those about being old, poor, rich, or female—we know it. We know what 'people could think.' We know that anything we do that fits the stereotype could be taken as confirming it" (5). Steele's *Whistling Vivaldi: How Stereotypes Affect Us and What We Can Do* is an accessible version of his extensive research on the ways that any suggestion that women, for example, are not good at math, actually reduces their performance due to increased anxiety about conforming to the stereotype and even internalizing it. Stereotype threat sets us up to fail because we're afraid that if we do falter, we only confirm the stereotype. I write about Steele's work more extensively in "To Write a Different Story: Reflective Reading as a Pedagogical Practice of Restorative Justice for Racial Oppression," a chapter in my book *Reflective Reading and the Power of Narrative: Producing the Reading*. There is actually quite a lot about teaching in that book, but Steele's work shows how important it is to attend to identity in the classroom:

> Hundreds of factors play into situations in which individuals feel identity threat: having a southern accent anywhere except the south, being a White man on the basketball court, being a conservative in a predominantly liberal faculty, being a woman in a STEM class, being African American in college . . . Steele's work is ultimately hopeful, because his experiments identify ways in which identity threat can be reduced: "if enough cues in a setting can lead members of a group to feel 'identity safe,' it might neutralize the impact of other cues in the setting that could otherwise threaten them" (Steele 147, in Sproles, *Reflective Reading* 57–58)

Steele reminds us that we are teaching individuals with any number of visible and unseen vulnerabilities. If they're busy protecting themselves, they'll have less energy and attention for learning. Since students' identities and our own are set before class even begins, we can take advantage of that by trying to connect with them beforehand. A welcoming email before the first day of class is a great way to open a connection and help them feel "identity safe." You can use the opportunity to introduce yourself, but I like to keep it simple by attaching the syllabus and, if we are online, sending information about how to log into class along with a short note saying that I'm looking forward to getting to know them. Another strategy for building community in the classroom is to meet with students in small groups, either in person or online. I use the second day of class for this. Students sign up in small groups for a 10-minute chat during the class period. Our task is to discuss their goals for the course in anticipation of creating learning objectives together in the next class, but it's also my way of getting to know them and introducing them to one another. I think it makes them more likely to talk to me individually about how things are going for them throughout the semester.

George Kuh's research demonstrates that students learn better when they are engaged. Christy Price in "Why Don't My Students Think I'm Groovy?" shows that students expect classes to be relevant and relaxed and for instructors to explain their rationale, establish a rapport, and use active learning. During a panel with students from the different service academies, Declan Harrison, then a senior at the Naval Academy, said, "A means to engender effective classroom engagement comes from students feeling connected with their instructor. Prior to class, having an instructor ask how students are doing and what is going on in their lives outside of the classroom lets the students know their professor cares about them. Students are able to gain an appreciation that their professors care about them when they ask questions that are not all focused on academics." I have heard this countless times from students in the mid-semester feedback (FACT) sessions I conduct.

When I reported to an instructor teaching online for the first time that students appreciated informal chatting at the start of class, he expressed surprise because his students appeared not to have responded to his inquiries about how they were doing. As it turned out, even though he was getting crickets, the students were indeed responding, by realizing that he cared about their well-being. Although he didn't feel the connection, they did. Research shows that engaged students learn more effectively, but how can we create an inclusive and engaging classroom climate? Some of the ways to do that are counterintuitive.

Faculty are typically surprised that students are disturbed by other students texting and checking email in class. They appreciate instructors who have a policy of no technology unless it's related to class. They also say cold calling keeps them on their toes. As Declan noted, "Instructors randomly calling on students in the virtual environment kept everyone engaged as they did not want to be the Midshipman that wasn't prepared, or even worse, didn't hear the question asked." Not all students feel this way, however. I ask students to discuss a question in pairs before calling on them. This gives the introverts time to think, and it gives everyone a bit of cover to be able to say "We thought . . ." or "We were confused."

Whether you'll be teaching online or in person or, as I was at the time of this writing, in a hybrid model with some students in the classroom and others Zooming from quarantine, consider what active learning is going to look like in your classes as you're conceiving your courses. Consider, for example, how to mitigate stereotype threat—there's a list of ways to do this in "Workshops"—and how to make good use of the first day of class. Start as you mean to continue. If you're going to work in groups, do that on the first day. If you expect discussion, do that on the first day. It's only fair to let students know what they'll be doing during the semester and what you expect of them in class. I lean heavily on discussion pairs, so that's what we do on the first day. I have found that pairs work regardless of whether we're online or socially distanced in the classroom (although, in the latter case, things get really loud).

Regan Gurung and Noelle Galardi make the important point that a warm and welcoming tone in the syllabus encourages students to ask questions and come to office hours. No matter how warm the tone, however, by all means don't just read the syllabus and then dismiss the class. This is where the idea of the "promising syllabus" comes in. Ken Bain discusses it in *What the Best College Teachers Do* (74–75), and James Lang looks at it in his article "The Promising Syllabus." The idea is to avoid "syllabus day" by making promises rather than announcing the policies. I have a scavenger hunt during the next class to make sure students have read the syllabus. They review the syllabus in pairs to find a dozen crucial pieces of information, such as how to contact the instructor and when the first paper is due. I call this a scavenger hunt instead of a quiz—one of many ways to lower the stakes for the activity and thus lower the chances of students feeling stereotype threat. Seriously, they have been reading for quite a while by this point; they don't need me to read the syllabus to them. Here's how I introduce my "Forms of Poetry" class on the first day:

This course promises to help you to

- Scan poetry and appreciate how a deep understanding of the structure of poetry leads to critical interpretation.
- Read poems closely.
- Understand the genre of poetry.
- Write critically about poetry.
- Identify poetic movements: medieval, Renaissance, neo-classical, Romantic, Victorian, modernist, and contemporary.
- Join the conversation of critical responses to poetry.

This course will fulfill its promises by asking you to

- Participate in class and in the design of the course.
- Work cooperatively with your partner.
- Complete and think about the assigned reading prior to class.
- Write, rewrite, and reflect on your writing.
- Respond to your partner's writing about literature—and work together to figure out how to improve everyone's work.

Then I ask the class what they are hoping to get out of the course, and we add their expectations as an appendix to the syllabus. I have been surprised by some of the things they suggest. One class wanted to memorize a couple of poems. Another wanted to write poems of their own. One time a student said he wanted to rediscover his love of reading.

When we're in person and can exchange papers, I use a card-swapping exercise called the Game of 35 to form a consensus on the expectations they want to add. (See "Workshops" for the rules of the game.) I also use the Game of 35 to develop a class statement on academic honesty. In this instance, I create an online Google doc that the students work on together. It's great to do this on the first day of class, as the perfect ice breaker. Students have to talk to each other, plus it has a purpose.

One of the many things I love about the Game of 35 is that it engages all students regardless of their intersectional identities. I am constantly searching for learning activities that do that. The most important thing, I've found, is finding a way to connect with students individually. The best time to do so is just before class. Getting there five minutes early is optimal, regardless of whether you're online or in person, in the classroom or waiting in the hallway. You can chat with students informally as they arrive, but the most important thing is just to be available.

In *Advice for New Faculty Members*, Boice makes the excellent point that students' stereotype of professors is that we are distant, too busy for them, more concerned with our research than our teaching, and generally unapproachable. In his studies on the causes of student incivilities—which he defines as ranging from not taking notes or asking questions to cheating on exams—he discovered that students are more inclined to behave badly if "teachers' negativities confirmed students' skepticism" (87). The "negativities" he found include teachers "perceived as distant, cold, and uncaring (i.e., lacking in immediacy)" and giving "fast-paced, noninvolving lectures" that distanced them from students (86). These are particularly problematic for women, who, as Kate Manne shows in *Down Girl: The Logic of Misogyny*, are punished for not being nurturing.

My colleague Matt Hawks was concerned about developing a rapport with his students. A naval officer and naturally quiet, Matt knew that he could be perceived as distant and uncaring. On top of that, he teaches a required course in statistics that not everyone is excited to be taking. To increase engagement, he decided to start each class with "The Daily Question." It takes a bit of time, but the results are worth it. He has to develop a long list of diverse questions, ranging from "What was your first paying job?" to "What was something you had to learn the hard way?" In my classes, I start Fridays by asking students what made them happy that week. Students love Matt's Daily Question. I found that I loved it too when Matt and I used it to kick off our small group discussions during new faculty orientation. Matt gave a presentation on it—"The Daily Question: Building Student Trust and Interest in Your Course"—at USNA's Third Annual Conference on Teaching and Learning (May 2018). The slides from the presentation include lists of questions. (See "References" for web access to Matt's presentation.)

The last thing I will say about active learning is that my goal is 100 percent student engagement. Even in the liveliest discussion, some students will be unprepared; one student will be talking; some will be listening, but most are passive (or at best preparing for what they're going to say). I have found that the key is small groups—two or three students being ideal. Think-pair-share is also excellent. Even in large classes, students can turn to one another in pairs or groups of three. When they're talking together, that's the 100 percent engagement I'm looking for, and because they have time to reflect, it's a perfect way to encourage introverts to participate.

I know many wonderful teachers who throw themselves headlong into the classroom and use every ounce of energy and charisma to pull their students through difficult material. I loved teachers like that—they were performers as well as educators—but I knew I couldn't be that teacher. I had to find another way. I'm grateful that I did. Research shows that moving yourself to tears during a lecture is not the best way to get students to learn; just because you feel engaged during class doesn't mean that they do. Also, it's exhausting and overstimulating. After a full day of teaching like that, it's hard to do anything else.

To find a model for yourself, watch others teach, but don't pretend to be "great teacher X" if that's just not you. Don't be intimidated by the person who taught the course before you; you are a different person, and you will teach a different class. You need to find out who you are in the classroom so you can build authentic relationships with students. I urge you to rely on pedagogy instead of your own energy in the classroom. You are going to need that energy for the next chapters.

How to Connect with Students

- Go to class early for informal conversations.
- Get to know your students and what their learning objectives are for the course.
- Mitigate stereotype threat.
- Use active learning to engage students.
- Understand how the brain learns and make sure students understand your pedagogical choices.
- Think about how you're going to teach something as much as what you're going to teach, and challenge yourself to develop active learning strategies to engage your students.

If You Are New to Teaching

- Know that you will get better.
- Be patient with yourself.
- Be compassionate toward your students.
- Keep a growth mindset: you might not know how to teach . . . yet.
- Read Principle 1, Face Down Impostor Syndrome, as often as you need to.

Want to learn more? I recommend the following:

Ambrose, Susan, et al. *How Learning Works: 7 Research-Based Principles for Smart Teaching.*
Brent, Rebecca, and Richard Felder. *Teaching and Learning STEM: A Practical Guide.*
Lang, James. "The Promising Syllabus."
———. *Small Teaching: Everyday Lessons from the Science of Learning.*
Neuhaus, Jessamyn. *Geeky Pedagogy: A Guide for Intellectuals, Introverts, and Nerds Who Want to Be Effective Teachers.*
Weimer, Maryellen. *Learner-Centered Teaching: Five Key Changes to Practice.*

PRINCIPLE 6

Reflect on Teaching
and Student Evaluations

I'M GUESSING THAT YOU REFLECT on your teaching after every class. I know I do, but I also recognize that such reflection is often deceiving. There are things that I surmise about how prepared the students were, for example, but mostly my reflection is based on how I feel. Did I have a lot of energy, or was I dragging? Was I pleased with something one of the students said? Did I feel connected to the students? How brilliant was I? None of these thoughts, however, help me understand the experience my students had. While you should seek out varying ways to gauge what your students (as well as your peers) think about your teaching, student evaluations—not always easy to stomach—are the most regular source of information about their experience, for better or worse.

Student evaluations serve an important role because there are certain things that only students can tell us about a course. Did they receive timely and constructive feedback? Was the atmosphere in the classroom conducive to learning? Were they treated with respect? Was the instructor available outside of class? Unfortunately, most of the student evaluations I've reviewed ask students to comment on things they're in no position to judge. How could they possibly know whether the instructor was knowledgeable about the subject or included appropriate material? How can they assess their own learning? Students tend to conflate effort with quality, and if they worked hard on something, they expect a high grade. That doesn't always work out for them, and their frustration often shows up in the evaluations in one way or another.

Another thing students likely don't know is the importance of their evaluations. At some institutions, student evaluations are the only way teaching is assessed. Be sure to let your students know how your institution uses student evaluations and assure them that you take them seriously, too. Show it by giving students time at the beginning of a class to fill them out. This also ensures that you'll get evaluations from a good percentage of the class. I tell my classes to take as much time as they need to complete the form. They never take more than 15 or 20 minutes, and I get fulsome comments.

As soon as the evaluation forms become available, I ask students to fill them out. I started doing this because I thought I'd get richer responses if they hadn't already done evaluations for their other classes, but it turns out there's an even better reason: A student worker who attended my "Preparing for P&T" workshop told me that he was surprised at how important student evaluations are in the promotion and tenure process. He said, "I don't think students take them seriously. They come at the end of the last day of classes, and we just want to get out of there. We just dash something off so that we can leave early." Yikes.

Once you've read your student evaluations, it's important to frame them by putting them into context and reflecting on what you can learn from them. The best way to do this is to read them with someone who can help you put them in perspective. Ask a mentor, or trade evaluations with a colleague. Someone else can help you appreciate the positive comments that are easy to ignore because you're focusing on the negative ones. The more your evaluations are exposed to the light, the less personal they will feel. Reading someone else's evaluations will help you understand your own. You can see that a zinger might be a sign of disgruntlement and therefore begin to think about how to address valid criticism, which sometimes takes a while to decipher. It takes thought and practice to read between the lines, but it's worth it if you really want to improve student learning.

It took me years to figure out what was behind a seemingly inexplicable comment I received during the second half of the British Literature Survey course: "Prof. Sproles is rude. She doesn't mean to be, but she's just naturally arrogant." That is not how people tend to describe me. It was a real head scratcher. None of the colleagues I discussed it with could figure it out. While other students wrote that I was caring and compassionate, one student had clearly had a different experience. Reading my evaluations with colleagues helped me see that this was a one-off that I shouldn't take as defining. That was helpful, but several years later I got a similar comment in the same course. What was I doing every once in a while to alienate one student in the class? It wasn't until a teaching workshop on how to ask questions that I figured it out. Forgive me for using a literature-specific example here, but trust me, there's a point to it.

I begin the course with Wordsworth's "Tintern Abby" and ask the class, "What is the meter and rhyme scheme of the poem?" (a question addressed at length in the anthology's introduction to the poem). The answer is blank verse. There's a regular meter but no rhyme scheme. I begin the course this way deliberately because I wanted to place "Tintern Abby" at the fulcrum between the highly structured rhyme schemes that previously dominated British poetry and the near abandonment of structure in modernist poetry's free verse. I used this poem to exemplify my course-long argument that the literary canon consists of works that intervene in current literary conventions and influence subsequent writers. It's challenging for students to understand literary history.

The example I cite above serves as a touchstone for the rest of the semester, and really, I pose the question rhetorically, always being prepared to answer it myself as an introduction to the history of rhyme and meter in British poetry. With sections of forty-five students, I only nominally expect discussion anyway. What I realized in the teaching workshop was that in my classes there had been two young men, who proud of their English major's knowledge of the subject, had confidently answered my question with the incorrect response of "free verse." In both cases, I was surprised to get a response at all, but delighted that it played perfectly into my plan for the day by giving me the opening to say, "No! It's blank verse. Let's look at the difference." What to me had seemed like a lucky teachable moment was actually a moment of public humiliation for these two young men, who probably never spoke up in class again. They had started off as eager allies, but now, because of my focus on the material instead of their learning, they were sullen foes.

Thinking about those two comments had a huge impact on my teaching. Now in that course I say, "Turn to your neighbor and take a look at the introduction to the poem; see if you can find a description of the structure of the poem." It might seem like a small change, but it signals early on in the course that I'm not going to ask "gotcha" questions that potentially expose the students' failure to do the reading or figure out what is significant about assignments they can't decipher. It shows the students that I am their guide, not their quizmaster. This realization has changed the way I set up discussions in every class I teach.

This is the sort of reflection on student evaluations that demonstrates that you're truly engaged in continual improvement and are open to making significant changes that will increase student learning. Some departments ask faculty for a written reflection on student evaluations at the end of the year, but even if yours doesn't, it's a good idea to do it anyway. You can include it in your annual evaluation and in the teaching portfolio—a collection of examples of your teaching effectiveness—that you submit for tenure and promotion. There's much more on teaching portfolios in Principle 8.

In addition to allowing you to demonstrate that you can learn from taking on student feedback, the teaching portfolio also helps balance student evaluations with other evidence of your teaching effectiveness by including course materials, observations from peers, and your own reflections on your teaching. But even the most carefully curated teaching portfolio can't completely negate consistently negative student evaluations. Remember that the members of your promotion and tenure committee are also instructors who have been reading their own student evaluations for years as well as lots of other people's. They should be able to tell when a student is writing out of anger, even when clever enough to couch their criticism in terms that appear valid.

I once received an evaluation that appeared calculated to get me fired on the spot: I was unprepared for class, wasted their time with pointless peer workshops, assigned so much reading that the entire class had given up on trying to do it, and was inconsistent in my grading. It was obvious to me that this had come from a student who sat right in front of me emitting a toxic fugue. I discourage people from trying to figure out who wrote which evaluation, but in this case, it was perfectly clear, because the student had refused to participate in peer reviews, deeming them a waste of time since he didn't trust anyone's opinion of his writing except his own. He didn't do the reading, a fact reflected in the grades he earned on the reading checks and exams. During my annual review, I asked the provost to read the evaluation and help me understand what was going on there. "Clearly," he said, "he wasn't doing the work and is lashing out at you." Ah. Could it be that he was angry that I held him accountable for doing the reading? I later heard from a colleague that the student referred to English classes as "book clubs." Many students think they can bullshit their way through English classes, but I had exposed him. I don't feel bad about it, but I wanted to provide some context to his comments.

Another example of comments that need contextualization are the bombs you're likely to get if you've discovered someone cheating. That person (and their friends) are likely to be especially nasty in the evaluations. Anyone reading them will need to know what motivated the firestorm, because I guarantee you the students won't say, "This is the worst class ever *because I got caught plagiarizing in it.*"

If there are consistent comments from multiple students that send up a red flag, you can't ignore them. Comments that suggest an instructor is disrespectful, creates a hostile learning environment, does not return work, or is unavailable need to be addressed immediately. When a faculty member becomes defensive and blames the students, I get worried. Peer observation can help clarify where the problem lies. Sometimes it requires that the faculty member reconsider their attitude toward the students. This is within your control. Sometimes, however, it requires students changing their attitude toward the faculty member. This is a more difficult problem.

I have often seen a pattern of negative comments stemming from unconscious bias. This is almost exclusively aimed at women, and in particular Black women. As Marlene Daut wrote in "Becoming Full Professor While Black":

> I was devastated to learn that the department had labeled me and the only other woman of color in my graduate-program cohort as bad teachers (based on inappropriate personal comments made on our course evaluations by students), thus leaving us ineligible for certain kinds of internal grants. As new instructors, we had little understanding of how our students' highly racialized perceptions of us as unintelligent, "mean," and undeserving of their respect were affecting our teaching evaluations in ways that our white male and female peers did not have to endure.

I have worked with many department chairs to help them see the misogyny and racism informing some students' evaluations. One enlightened chair, "Seymour," started a recent conversation by saying that he (a white man) thought that 30 percent of the comments a junior department member (a Black woman) had received were racist. He then described identical comments I'd read in other student evaluations of Black women. By the end of our conversation, he agreed that more like 95 percent of the comments were probably racist. The sorts of things I've read are well described by Kerry Ann Rockquemore and Tracey Laszloffy in *The Black Academic's Guide to Winning Tenure—without Losing Your Soul*:

> Because blackness is stereotypically associated with intellectual inferiority, students experience dissonance when they see a black person behind the podium. This results in an unconscious stance where the black professor must prove his or her credibility, intelligence, and experience to the students in the class and where the slightest perceived error will be read as

incompetence. White students regularly critique the competency of black faculty as teachers, challenge their authority aggressively in the classroom, question their legitimacy as scholars, fail to show the most basic level of respect, and express overly familiar communication styles and greetings (as if interacting with a peer) . . . In addition to the general questions of competence and differential treatment, white students may feel far more comfortable exercising their power over you as a black faculty member than over your white colleagues. This can take the form of going "over your head" to complain about your teaching to a higher authority figure such as a department head or dean (who is typically white and male). *Students may also attempt to exert their power through end-of-semester evaluations where they critique black faculty more harshly, are less tolerant of black faculty who are tough in grading and strict with discipline, and are more likely to penalize black professors for being academically rigorous (particularly in courses where race relations are part of the course content).* (18; emphasis added)

I sent this quotation to Seymour, and he replied, "Point taken. I just ordered the book."

Students' implicit biases can have devastating consequences. In the conversation I had with Seymour, the first concern was the impact of the negative evaluations on the junior faculty member, who was seriously considering resigning. Our next concern was how to ensure that members of the promotion and tenure committee be able to see the evaluations as racist smears rather than reliable testimony. I recommended a strategy that had worked well in the past: the chair sits in on a course for a semester and thus can attest that the students' criticisms are baseless. I urged the chair to use this opportunity to show deference and respect to the faculty member in front of students, thus using his unearned authority to confer status on her. Though time-consuming, this is an effective way to support a faculty member who's being undermined by student opinion. The chair, through personal experience, bears witness to the faculty member's effectiveness in the classroom, and that cannot be challenged. If you don't have a chair who's willing to do this for you, ask a colleague to sit in on classes and report to the chair.

I wish we didn't have to address the potential for student evaluations to be hurtful and sometimes even vicious as the result of internalized racism and misogyny. If you've ever received a spite-bomb at the end of the semester, it's crucial that you know you're not alone. Not by a long shot. It is so common for women to receive unjustified negative comments that, if this hasn't happened to you, you belong to a fortunate minority. Let's consider a pre-COVID example that's still all too fresh in my mind.

"Susan" came to my office at the end of the semester holding her student evaluations like they were a pile of writhing cobras that might strike at any moment. "I know this is childish," she said, "but I just got my student evaluations, and I wonder if I can just sit in your office to read them. I don't want to interrupt you. I just don't want to be alone with them." This is not an uncommon occurrence. I invite colleagues to read their evaluations with me. I know how hurtful some of the comments can be and that one or two personal, negative remarks can stick with you for years. My oldest daughter is approaching 30, but I still remember the evaluation I received the semester she was born. Those were the days before parental leave (which I might have mentioned a few times already).

My daughter was obligingly born the Friday of spring break, and I was back in the classroom the following Monday morning—after 24 hours of back labor and no sleep to speak of—returning a batch of essays. I taught an evening seminar that semester and had one student who could only meet at the end of class. Meanwhile, I'm nursing a colicky newborn and finding it difficult to make it through the three-hour seminar without leaking, much less a paper conference afterward. Oh, and did I mention that this was the semester I was up for tenure? Ultimately, the student and I agreed to talk by phone. And the student's evaluation? "Prof. Sproles is never available. It's almost like she loves her baby more than she loves us." Almost? Seriously?

I have a Black colleague whom a student described as "sassy." In another instance, Susan—an American of Middle Eastern heritage who is often thought to be Latina and who looks younger than she is—received comments in her student evaluations about having difficulty understanding her because of her "foreign accent." Honestly? She's from Seattle. The most hurtful (and inappropriate) comments are about physical appearance. I've seen complaints that professors don't wear makeup or that they have jiggling arm flab. I have read thousands of student evaluations.

Men don't get comments like these. Numerous studies prove that women receive evaluations lower than men. This is particularly true in required classes, where everyone's evaluations are lower than in major classes and electives. Regardless, for women they remain lower. I have colleagues who don't read their student evaluations because the negative comments so demoralize them. In *Down Girl: The Logic of Misogyny*, Kate Manne explains, "As a professor, you have to stand before a crowd and ask them to invest in your words in the coin of trust, respect, and attention. And it turns out that gender has a significant impact both on how, and how well, you are subsequently evaluated . . . Joey Sprague and Kelley Massoni (2005) showed that male professors are penalized more for being boring, and female professors for seeming cold, uncaring, or not developing a personal relationship with each and every student" (267).

I have noticed a pattern in the comments women receive that stems, I believe, from deep-rooted assumptions that women are (or should be) nurturing, caring, and compassionate. These prejudices are reinforced by cultural assumptions about women and mothering, best described by Nancy Chodorow in *The Reproduction of Mothering*—which, like Manne's more recent book, makes for a sobering read. It is difficult for some students to reconcile expectations that a woman should be nurturing with the reality that in the classroom she is an authority figure. Women's attempts to assert this authority frequently backfire. Typical comments about women's teaching include these:

She was condescending.
She was demeaning when talking to us at times.
She makes it known that she knows more than us.
She is full of herself.

Comments like this are an indication of "negative mother transference," to use the psychoanalytic term. When we are not sufficiently motherly, we get punished. For BIPOC women, this is a particularly awful bind. You lack credibility as the result of racist bias, and if you assert your credentials, you're not nurturing as the result of sexist bias.

While you might think it a given that professors know more about the subjects they teach than their students, this doesn't always seem to be appreciated by the students. The mid-semester feedback sessions I've conducted through the FACT program have allowed me to ask students what they mean when they say a female instructor is condescending or demeaning. They responded that the instructor uses words they don't understand. Now, this seems to me like the opposite of condescending, but I think students just don't know how to describe how uncomfortable they feel when a woman exhibits intellectual authority. When describing the same behavior in male instructors, they say, "He's too smart for us; he needs to dumb it down; what he says goes over our heads." Notice the difference here: The students willingly concede that the male instructor knows more about the subject than they do, and their constructive advice is to unpack that knowledge by defining unfamiliar words. This is good advice. We all forget what it was like before we became experts in our fields, but I don't see men being criticized personally for this. They are not described as condescending or demeaning; it is assumed that they are more knowledgeable. Women are not granted this respect; we are showing off.

I asked Susan to read her evaluations aloud to me since, as I mentioned earlier, it is enormously useful to read them with someone who isn't going to respond to them the way we cannot help but respond to our own. Out of a class of 25, 21 students had completed evaluations. Many included glowing comments, such as "this is the best professor I have ever had." One was negative but constructive, the student framing their criticism within the context of their own failure to perform. Two were vicious and easily four times longer than the others. Both evaluations were quite similar, suggesting the students had discussed them beforehand. They described Susan as "emotional," "doesn't like us; negative attitude," "complained that we were not doing our work properly and never gave us feedback." It was clear that the two of them expected to receive poor grades and wanted to make it Susan's fault. I found it easy to see through their complaints. Because some students see us as "mothers," they perceive our feedback as complaints and view grades as a sign of whether we like them. This leads them to respond to our assessments as if they're being punished rather than educated. Often it's the female students who fail to recognize these boundaries and see a woman with power as a threat who needs to be taken down a peg.

An interesting wrinkle in Susan's case pointed to another dynamic that affects women. Some of her students were working on projects co-facilitated by a male colleague who consistently supported Susan's judgment. They still struggled, but they accepted her feedback. Another group had a co-facilitator who questioned Susan's judgment and criticized her in front of the students; with her authority systematically undermined, it's no wonder the students resisted her criticism and felt invited to attack her personally. Both of her co-facilitators were male, but I don't think that mattered as much as one might think; I have seen similar situations in which a senior woman has been just as abusive to a junior female colleague. Among women in higher education, seniority is often read as authority, which leads to difficulty for younger women as teachers and in mid-career leadership roles.

Susan's story had a happy ending: both of the students she suspected of writing the negative evaluations contacted her after the course to thank her for holding them to high standards; they could already see it paying off in job interviews. Regardless, their evaluations were already on file. Susan and I worked together to put the evaluations in context for the promotion committee. After that, I got an email from another woman in Susan's department asking if she could come talk to me about her evaluations.

After visiting hundreds of classrooms and reading thousands of teaching evaluations, I can attest that men and women do receive markedly different comments, just as studies show. Those about white women and BIPOC women tend to be more personal and more critical. Having recognized that students describe women as condescending and men as smart, I found that my talks with students during mid-semester feedback sessions only reinforced that similar behaviors by men and women are often described in different ways:

Behavior	When by a man	When by a woman
Checking in (e.g., by asking, "Is that clear?")	Cares about student learning	Lacks confidence
Explaining a difficult subject	Talks over our heads	Is condescending
Making jokes	Has a dry sense of humor	Is sarcastic or, worse, sassy
Emphasizing the subject matter	Shows enthusiasm	Is emotional
Responding hours later, rather than immediately, after receiving an email	Is really busy	Is unavailable
Appearing distant	Is hard to read	Doesn't like me

Use this table to translate student comments into statements that are less loaded and misogynistic when summarizing your (or a colleague's) evaluations for your chair, annual review, or promotion and tenure package.

I want to pay particular attention to students' conclusions that we don't like them, because I think this cuts both ways. I think we often assume students don't like *us* when often it's more likely that they are afraid we don't like *them*. This is another situation that can lead to negative mother transference. If students see you as a mother figure, they will blame you if you can't fix everything—especially their grades. As I've noted, because they can't assess their own learning, they confuse it with effort. A comment on one of my student evaluations complained that my grading was unreliable because they had received a lower grade on a paper that they had spent the most time on. They clearly wanted an A for effort.

Comments resulting from negative mother transference tend to be more insistent, emphatic, and extreme. It's likely that they are driven by the student's anxiety about their grade. The comments also tend to be especially hurtful, because the student is trying to find a way to blame you for their own lack of success. This was definitely an issue for me when I first started teaching, but it is less of one now that I'm closer in age to my students' mothers. One reason is that I've learned to manage the transference, by becoming aware of my countertransference and not responding maternally. Another is that as I grew older,

I started looking more like an authority figure. I also rose in status. My colleagues treated me with greater respect, and that set an example for the students.

As I've previously emphasized, don't allow your student evaluations to become the primary source for evaluating you as a teacher. At the Naval Academy, we've been working hard to educate department chairs and members of the promotion and tenure committee about the racism and misogyny inherent in student evaluations, and I hope this is being done on your campus, too. A Google search for "student evaluations" will yield plenty of articles on this topic more current than any bibliography I could include here. As of early 2022, "Evaluating Student Evaluations of Teaching: A Review of Measurement and Equity Bias in SETs and Recommendations for Ethical Reform," by Rebecca J. Kreitzer and Jennie Sweet-Cushman, is the most comprehensive review of the research on student evaluations. It concludes that evaluations do indeed contain bias against white women and BIPOC faculty—but it's complicated. The authors emphasize the importance of using multiple measures to assess teaching instead of overreliance on student perceptions.

Because of the sheer number of pages of student evaluations, they are likely to literally outweigh all of the other evidence chairs and tenure committees read about your teaching. Counterbalance their impact with reflections on your teaching, which are especially impactful when couched in response to mid-semester and end of the semester feedback. If your institution has a formal process for obtaining mid-semester feedback from students, that's fantastic. If not, you can partner with a colleague to do a Formative Analysis of Classroom Teaching (FACT) (described in "Workshops") for each other. You can also get anonymous feedback yourself by asking the class what they think you should start doing, stop doing, and continue doing. It is essential to respond to mid-semester feedback by making the changes suggested or explaining why that can't be done. I'm not saying this will fix your student evaluations, but it will most likely help. Sometimes it is just a matter of explaining something to students that you thought they understood.

At the end of one semester, several students complained about the disorganization of the Google Classroom site. I realized they were viewing the "Stream" tab instead of the "Coursework" tab, which is where class material is organized by topic. I showed them how to get to the "Coursework" tab, which I think probably helped them in other classes as well. There were still complaints in my student evaluations about the disorganization of Google Classroom, but all but one of them went on to say that I had fixed the problem after they pointed it out to me. Sigh.

At the Naval Academy, we have seen enormous value when faculty members briefly summarize each set of their own evaluations with a final note providing relevant context and reflection on how they plan to address any concerns. Sound out your department and tenure committee about this approach. You could also ask your chair or mentor to review your student evaluations and summaries and write a note confirming that the summaries are an accurate reflection of the evaluations.

In addition to your own reflections, include peer observations in your teaching portfolio. If your department doesn't have a system for doing this early on in your appointment, engage a mentor or colleague to observe your classes at least once a year and write an evaluation for your portfolio and for you to respond to as part of your reflective teaching practice. Most class observations I've read—and until recently those I've conducted—have tended to be narrative observations that carefully avoid any criticism or recommendations for improvement. This is the equivalent of readers who comment that your article is interesting, but then don't provide the feedback you need to ensure publication.

The most effective model I have seen for getting useful feedback on teaching is the Paired Peer Observation system, piloted by Rebecca Brent and Richard Felder at North Carolina State University. In this model, two of your colleagues talk with you about your goals for a course and then together observe your class. During their visit, they each fill out an evaluation sheet that Brent and Felder have thoroughly vetted over the years. After class, the two observers work together to complete a third, combined evaluation sheet that they'll then present to you. There are enormous advantages to this system:

- It forces the observers to actually evaluate what they see.
- The categories on the evaluation form emphasize pedagogy rather than content (I cannot tell you how many times I've talked to observers who evaluated "teaching" based on how interested they were in the content of the class.)
- The norming experience of coming to agreement on a shared evaluation means that the observers have to support and defend their assessments to one another. Thus, any imbalances in observation come to light. If the two can't agree on something, they average the score. (When I did this exercise in one of Brent and Felder's workshops, I was shocked to discover what a hard grader I was.)
- Because observers must articulate their impressions, implicit biases are mitigated or exposed.
- The shared evaluation gives each observer cover; it is much easier to say "We noticed . . ." than "I think . . ."
- The evidence supplied through this system is so credible and robust that it goes a long way toward counterbalancing student evaluations.
- It provides a powerful source for your own reflection, especially if you can point to positive changes observed in subsequent class visits.
- It demonstrates your dedication to your teaching and your desire to seek to improve.

How to Reflect on Your Teaching and Student Evaluations

- Read them with a colleague.
- Summarize them at the end of each semester and note the changes you plan to make as a result; reflect on those changes after the next semester.

- Be aware of implicit biases against women—and especially BIPOC women.
- Try not to take them personally.
- Balance their impact with peer observations: collect and respond to mid-semester feedback and a paired peer observation.

Want to learn more? I recommend the following:

Brent, Rebecca, and Richard Felder. "A Protocol for Peer Review of Teaching."

Daut, Marlene L. "Becoming Full Professor While Black."

Kreitzer, Rebecca J., and Jennie Sweet-Cushman. "Evaluating Student Evaluations of Teaching: A Review of Measurement and Equity Bias in SETs and Recommendations for Ethical Reform."

Rockquemore, Kerry Ann, and Tracey Laszloffy. *The Black Academic's Guide to Winning Tenure—without Losing Your Soul.*

PRINCIPLE 7

Make Scholarship a Habit

I AM PASSIONATE ABOUT TEACHING, but my research is central to my identity. I can imagine not teaching, but I wouldn't be me if I weren't a scholar. Research drew me to graduate school in the first place, so I can't imagine my life without it. That doesn't mean it always comes easily though. In fact, sometimes it can be downright agonizing. When I was trying to complete my dissertation, I made a deal with myself out of desperation that I had to sit at a computer without an Internet connection every day from 8:00 a.m. to 10:00 a.m. I didn't have to write during that time, I just had to sit there; I couldn't do anything else—no email, no reading, no class prep, no grading. My plan worked like a charm.

It turned out that the only thing worse than writing up my research was sitting for two hours doing nothing. The main reason my strategy worked was that after a few days of locking myself in, working from 8:00 to 10:00, got to be a habit. I'm not suggesting that you do the same, but you do need to find a way to sustain your scholarship no matter where you are in your career. I know you're busy, but take a hard look at the excuses you make to avoid research, and then figure out how to build scholarship into your schedule.

New faculty members often justify putting off scholarship for two reasons. The first reason is deciding not to worry about research or writing until they feel they have their teaching responsibilities under control. In most cases, they do this on the advice of their dissertation committee members. This is especially common for new faculty taking up positions at small, teaching-oriented schools. Don't listen to this advice. No matter how great the mentors on your dissertation committee are, they likely know little about the expectations at your new institution—even if it's another R1. If you get the same advice at your new institution, don't listen to that either.

When I arrived at a small liberal arts college with a teaching focus, the dean told me that teaching mattered above all else, but that I should still do some research "to feel better about myself." I was surprised and a bit discouraged at the suggestion that the institution didn't value scholarship. As a graduate student, I had keenly felt the comments that I was a good teacher, which dismissively implied that I wasn't a serious scholar. I suspected at the time that such remarks were largely misogynistic, informed by the notion that women should be caring and not intellectually threatening. I have since heard similar stories from other women who were discouraged from doing research and encouraged to think of themselves as teachers. My new institution apparently shared that attitude.

I quickly noticed that the most respected faculty members there were the most successful scholars—white men all. Fortunately, I didn't listen to that dean's advice, and when a new dean was hired from outside the institution, she came with a very different idea about the publications needed for tenure. If I hadn't continued publishing and presenting at conferences on my own initiative, I would've been sunk. (There will be more on the vagaries of tenure expectations in the next principle.) What's more, even if I had gotten tenure, I would have been stuck.

When I got that first job, I fully expected to keep it until I retired, but after 10 years, my personal and professional goals had shifted. Having had children, I wanted to be closer to family. After chairing the department, I sought bigger administrative challenges. Had I not been an active scholar, I wouldn't have made a viable candidate for another position elsewhere. So the lesson learned is that even if you're at a teaching institution, don't listen to insinuations that your scholarship doesn't matter. Regardless of whether scholarship is integral to your identity, it will allow you to keep your options open if you decide you want to leave.

I didn't listen to the first dean because I wanted to be part of an intellectual community that valued both scholarship and teaching. Even if you feel a sense of community at your institution, your scholarship connects you to an even larger community outside its walls. No matter how genial the institution is, it will feel claustrophobic at times. At my first job, I wanted to be valued as a scholar as well as a teacher because it felt to me like a recursive relationship. It turns out, there's research making just this point.

Robert Boice found that new faculty who focused on writing had better teaching evaluations than new faculty who focused on teaching (101). Of note, Boice and others typically use "writing" as a substitute for all kinds of research. In my field, writing is mostly what we do, but in others writing is just a small part of the research process. In some fields, scholarship is measured by publications, but in others it's productions or exhibitions that matter. Boice's revelation about "writing" applies equally to all forms of research, including grant writing and creative projects. His finding that a focus on scholarship improves teaching makes sense to me because I know that when I'm engaged in research, I'm also more engaged in the classroom.

Students can tell when the material I'm presenting energizes me, which especially happens when I bring insights from my own work into the classroom. Share your work with your students. They have no idea about so many things. For instance, they don't know what academics do outside the classroom or that we're creating the knowledge that they're learning and that you are part of an intellectual community (and by the way, they'll respect you for that if they see that you have authority in your field). They also likely fail to realize that their textbooks are not handed down from on high, but are instead the products of scholars like us. They probably cannot see that what they're learning has relevance on a broader scale, with applications and connections beyond themselves and the classroom. They need to see you as a model for the scholars they might one day become, and themselves as the lifelong learners we want them all to be.

You have an opportunity to inspire your students—particularly your female and BIPOC students—by helping them to see that there is a path into academia for them. Talk with them about the path you took, so they can imagine an academic future for themselves. Introduce your students to the language of research by telling them about your own. Demystify it for them.

After I told my class about this book, they asked if they could read it. One student asked me how I kept up with my writing, and I told her some of the tips I share in this chapter—mainly to do a little every day and have lots of accountability groups. Another student asked about other books I had written, and then someone asked whether I enjoyed writing this book the most. "I wouldn't say I am actually enjoying it," I replied. "But I am enjoying revising it, because I have a wonderful group of women reading each chapter and giving me feedback. I love incorporating their responses into each chapter. They always make it a better book. It is much easier to write when you can imagine the people who are going to read your work." This conversation was the perfect introduction to the next class: a peer review workshop on the first draft of their papers. I promise you—your students will appreciate the subject matter and you more if they're let into the workings of your field, and you will benefit from the deeper integration of your scholarship into your teaching. So, no matter what you're told, keep up your research.

Another reason not to put your scholarship on hold is that it's harder than you think to get back to it after a hiatus. This brings me to the second mistake I often see new faculty make: waiting for summer. It's common to believe you need long stretches of uninterrupted time before you can even begin to think about scholarship. Waiting for the long stretches of time you imagine you'll have over the summer can cost you valuable start up time. By the time, you get back into a project that's been on hold for nine months, it'll be time to start preparing your fall classes. And let's not forget the interruptions of vacations, family obligations, deferred maintenance in the form of doctors' visits and all the other things you put off during the school year. I used to start making a spreadsheet in March to track a patchwork of summer camps to keep my children occupied. That expensive nightmare required so much management that it left me little time for research. Summer is not as long or as free as you might think.

Also, it is not necessary or even desirable to put off work until you have lots of time to focus on it. That was how many of us worked in graduate school, but it's not sustainable over a career. Boice studied faculty work habits and found that the most productive and successful faculty were those who worked at a steady, moderate pace (137–44). The teachers didn't work to exhaustion or wait for big blocks of free time or complain that teaching got in the way of the "important" work. Instead, they blocked off small amounts of time every day— sometimes as little as 15 minutes—to keep their research moving forward. In *Publish and Flourish*, Tara Gray offers the same advice—do a little bit every day. So does Gina Hiatt in "Why Writing Productively Is So Difficult, and What to Do about It." Yes, indeed. They all agree.

Protect your research time fiercely. As a woman, you will have to work harder in the classroom, plus women tend to get loaded down with service assignments, not to mention carrying the lion's share of housework and childcare. It is easier to protect your research time if you schedule small amounts of it on a daily basis. If you do have a research day, make good use of it. I have never been at an institution or in a position that allowed for a research day, but if I had, I would have scheduled two half days because having an hour (or two on a good day) first thing in the morning works best for me; I like it because I find that I am thinking about the project almost from the moment I get up. I have ideas in the shower and in the car. By the time I'm at the office, I've already begun to tackle research problems in my head; I no longer feel the hesitation or dread of trying to get going, because I'm excited about the new ideas and connections I've already begun to create. That's why you should make scholarship a habit.

My colleague, friend, and workout partner Samara Firebaugh put it this way: "The 'habit' framing also brings up a vast array of possible metaphors and analogies, as we are all happier when we have good habits even though it can be hard to wake up at 5:15 a.m. and jump into a pool when it's 55 degrees out (and that is so much easier to do when you've made a 'workout pact' with a friend . . .). Oh! the metaphors for habitual scholarship continue." True to Samara's observation, the good habit of scholarship makes me happier, and I suspect that you'll find that it cheers you up, too. It is so much easier to get back to a project you last touched 23 hours ago than one collecting dust. It becomes such a habit, you almost do it without thinking. As for a "workout pact" with a friend, we'll get to that in a bit, but when it comes to research, we can skip the icy water.

Boice's idea of brief daily sessions (BDS) is crucial for managing your time and working productively in any area of your life. Remember my example of "incremental gardening" in Principle 2? It's a good example of how BDS can work for class prep and research. Boice has studies to prove that scholars who work a little bit every day are more productive and successful in the long run than those who wait until they have days or weeks to binge before collapsing (144).

Doing a little research every day, even if only for five or ten minutes, keeps the work simmering so you don't lose time warming up to get back into it after a long pause. If you've done your planning, you will have mapped out the scope of the work so you can dip into it for a short period. Even if you don't have time to finish something, you have enough to get started. You will be amazed at how much you can accomplish in those five or ten minutes. Once you get used to working like this, what you can do in a thirty-minute session will amaze you. It will also be less painful, which means you're less likely to put it off. Stopping in the middle of something also helps you get back into the work. It's so much easier to pick something up than trying to figure out what to do next. I frequently leave myself notes about the next sentence, paragraph, or section of a project, so I can start the next day by following my own instructions.

My favorite trick is to open whatever I am working on first thing in the morning—after I've spent five minutes reviewing (or creating) priorities and a plan for the day. Ideally, I'll spend 30 minutes or an hour writing (sometimes two, if I'm lucky) because morning is when my mind is sharpest. Even if I find that I don't have time to do anything new, I'll try to spend at least five minutes reviewing the work I did the day before. After that, the document pops up throughout the day, jogging my memory about whatever it is I'm working on. Staying connected to your research pays dividends in allowing your brain to sometimes make connections and solve problems during moments of downtime.

Have you experienced a solution that suddenly comes to you while you're driving or going for a run or doing yoga? That was your resting brain continuing to work. As we learned in Principle 5, building neural pathways that connect new knowledge to existing knowledge happens during rest. Be deliberate about creating periods of rest so that your unconscious can do some of the heavy lifting. For that and several other reasons, take a five-minute break—deliberately—at least every 90 minutes when you're working. For your unconscious to assist in problem solving, though, you'll need to remain engaged in the problem. Even if you only have time to remind yourself what you're working on, do some research every day.

As Samara pointed out, it is also important to create some sort of accountability for yourself. If you work with collaborators, you form a natural accountability group. And, as my colleague and early reader Daphne Skipper advocates, be generous in acknowledging the people you work with even if they don't always hold up their end of the project. If you leave someone out, you're not only cutting them off, but also their network. If your work is solitary, make an effort to create external incentives for staying on track. For example, ask a colleague to partner with you to share plans and goals and help keep each other on track.

I have several accountability strategies, all involving other women, one of whom is my writing partner, Irene. In 2012 we started going to the library together every Friday morning to write. When we ended up in separate locations, we continued our weekly check-ins, but by phone. We've seen each other through the publication of a book each so far. This one will make three! Irene and I also participate in a daily BDS group started by our dear friend Katie Hogan. I have never physically met most of the women in this group, but I have followed their fascinating research careers through our daily (or not so daily) check-ins. All we do is report on how much time we have spent on our BDS. Here's an example of a report I made to the BDS group while working on this book: "90 minutes and then 45 minutes working on the fourth chapter of book on how women can succeed in higher ed. This is the section on time management, so I'm writing about Boice and describing the BDS group. I hope you all don't mind that I am claiming you all as my inspiration."

Once a week, I run a 30-minute writing group for faculty at my institution. This is an especially smart idea suggested by Scott Hottovy, a fellow Boice devotee. It works better for me that for anyone else because I'm obliged to be there. We used to meet in person, but since the pandemic we've gathered online. That works just fine. We turn on our cameras, mute ourselves, and start typing. Sometimes we share our goals for the session. We wave good-bye at the end, although many of us stay on longer than 30 minutes. This group helps me reset every week if I've been too distracted by grading or other things to work every day. It's easy to start any of these three ways to hold yourself accountable for your scholarship. I recommend doing all of them.

Clinical psychologist and academic writing coach Gina Hiatt's article "Why Writing Productively Is So Difficult, and What You Can Do about It" also directs us to Boice for guidance on maintaining scholarship. Hiatt includes a useful discussion of the many reasons why faculty struggle to complete research projects, including lack of deadlines (something conference papers can help overcome), no structure, being overwhelmed by urgent tasks (like teaching and service), negative reviews, reluctance to ask for help, little or no institutional support, and anxiety (which creates writer's block and avoidance). Like Boice, Hiatt recommends brief daily sessions, setting up accountability methods, and remembering that a draft doesn't have to be perfect. She also suggests that getting support from outside your institution might feel more comfortable, because it's more anonymous. Hiatt founded Academic Ladder Inc., which helps people complete and publish academic writing, and the web-based Academic Writing Club, to provide this type of support. I would suggest that if you pay for such assistance—which is a wise investment in your career—you'll find yourself more likely to follow through; you'll be more inclined to try to get the most you can out of it. This is one way to be accountable to yourself. Professionals pay for all kinds of services to help them succeed. As the poet Susan Facknitz pointed out when we were discussing this principle, Beyoncé gets her hair done. You also deserve to invest in yourself.

One of my favorite chapters in Boice is "Let Others Do Some of the Work," in which he recommends getting early feedback. When we were discussing this chapter in the weekly group I run for new faculty, Carolyn Judge, a naval architect, pointed out that I was modeling the practice of getting early feedback in the way I was writing this book. I hadn't thought of that! I asked Carolyn to describe the process she saw me using—thus doing some of the work for this chapter. (Thank you, Carolyn!). Here's what she wrote:

> As Karyn has worked on this book, I have seen both the benefits and the courage it takes to follow Boice's advice on early feedback. Karyn sends her chapters out to be read by women friends and colleagues as soon as the last word is written. The drafts always show lots of promise, but are often a bit disjointed or incomplete in the main point. She then gets feedback in various ways (including in-person group sessions—yikes!) where every weakness in the chapter is pointed out and dissected. During these (sometimes brutally) honest sessions, Karyn takes copious notes and asks questions to clarify choices and issues she is struggling with. After these sessions, I eagerly look forward to reading the revised draft. It is a wonder to me the way the words and structure change to fix all the original weaknesses. She will even cut the parts most dear to her if the case has been made that it doesn't add value to the chapter. The

quality of the final product is clearly directly related to the external input she solicits early on. I am inspired to be bolder in my requests for feedback and to be more emotionally heroic in accepting honest, constructive feedback.

I try, but I don't always take criticism gracefully. I also try to take it gratefully. Carolyn knows this. I often asked her to help me process the brutal comments she mentions. What I have learned over the years is that even responses that seem to have totally missed your point can be valuable. I frequently ignore the actual advice I'm given and instead ask myself, "What provoked that response?" It can be difficult to determine, but it is invariably worth it. Another advantage of having a group of women review each chapter as soon as it is drafted was that it gave me a clear sense of my audience, because, dear reader, I was writing it for you.

One of the hardest things about scholarship is knowing that after all the pain-staking work, it might not get accepted. Remember that there are lots of reasons your work might be rejected that have nothing to do with the work itself. It might not fit into the editorial plans for a journal or series. The editor might have recently accepted something on a similar topic or is trying to fill a specific gap. Anonymous readers might not like your subject, your tone, your critical perspective, your methodology. I often get reviews that make it clear the reviewer simply wanted a different book.

You probably won't know the reasons for many of the rejections you receive, but when you do get negative reviews, take a breath (or a week's worth of breaths). It stings. As with the advice I solicit from friendly readers, it's less important to take the advice than to figure out what provoked it. It is one thing to get advice from friends and colleagues, but quite another to receive it from reviewers. I have gotten my share of rejections, accompanied by scathing reviews. Tori Johnson, an ocean engineer, wrote to me about her experience:

One of the things that I wasn't prepared for when I started my academic career was how to handle very negative reviewer comments or paper rejections. Other than a vague conversation with my postdoc mentor, I was somewhat under the impression that professors "didn't" submit manuscripts that could get rejected. I have since learned (at least in my case) that is not true. This is the stuff that really stings and is hard to talk about, but ultimately I think that all of my failures have taught me to critically reevaluate my work, and I am so much prouder of the (eventual) final product. The hardest thing was reopening the document and having that initial conversation with my collaborators.

When responding to reviewers, the hardest thing for me to resist is pointing out why the reader is wrong. I've learned from experience that this will get you nowhere. Instead, try to figure out how to respond to reviews that addresses the readers' concerns without compromising your vision for the work. Asking a colleague to help you process criticism makes me feel exposed, but it's a great way to get some perspective. If you've gotten feedback early, those readers will have a vested interest in helping you figure out how to respond to negative comments.

That brings us to another chapter and important point from Boice—"Let Go of Negative Thoughts" and write mindfully. This is important not only when processing criticism, but also when internalizing criticism takes up valuable psychic space. Review Principle 2, Face Down Impostor Syndrome, as often as necessary to learn how to confront the source of the negative self-talk that diverts energy from your scholarship. And speaking of energy—you need it to think, as we learned from Baumeister and Tierney's *Willpower*. Principle 4, Manage Your Time, is particularly relevant when it comes to scholarship. Bring to bear on your research all of the things you learned in that chapter, including the knowledge that sometimes you just need a snack.

No matter how theoretical your work may be, your working habits need to be practical. Assess your circumstances and figure out how to intentionally build research into your day. We need to do research to help shape the future so it looks like us.

How to Make Scholarship a Habit

- Do a little every day, even 5–10 minutes.
- Open the most important document first thing in the morning, even if you don't have time to work on it then.
- Use the small bits of time in your day; start something even if you know you can't finish it.
- Stop in the middle of something so it's easy to pick it up the next time.
- Take a five-minute break—deliberately—at least every 90 minutes.
- Find accountability partners to share goals with and help keep each other on track.
- Get feedback early on.
- Manage negative emotions and internal critical voices; think three positive thoughts for every negative one.

Want to learn more? I recommend the following:

Boice, Robert. *Advice for New Faculty Members: Nihil Nimus.*
Gray, Tara. *Publish and Flourish: Become a Prolific Scholar.*
Hiatt, Gina. "Why Writing Productively Is So Difficult, and What to Do about It."
Silva, Paul. *How to Write a Lot.*

PRINCIPLE 8

Prepare for Promotion and Tenure Early

WHEN MY DAUGHTER PIPPA was in first grade, she came home one day talking about what she wanted to be when she grew up. I said, "What are you thinking about?" She said, "I'm not sure, but I know I want a job that leads to tenure."

No one needs to start preparing for promotion and tenure at 6 years of age, but it's a good idea to do so as soon as you're hired by becoming intimately familiar with departmental and institutional expectations for teaching, research, and service. As for some general advice before getting into the details of how to present your materials, be sure you understand the process and the timeline; know that most institutions value improvement in teaching, a clear research trajectory, some service for assistant professors, and quite a bit of service for associate professors; find out as much as you can about your department and institution's expectations by talking to the colleagues with whom you've made connections (but don't be surprised if they don't all agree); and ask your chair to help you distill your colleagues' advice into a plan for yourself. Last but not least, don't go through the process alone.

How is preparing for tenure different for women? In all the ways that other parts of higher education are different for them. Women have to make more of an effort to get the help we need. Part of that involves helping our male colleagues see and understand the misogyny and racism that undermine our authority in the classroom. We must also manage the larger burden of domestic labor and child-care, which eats into our research time. You know this list. The good news is that we can help each other overcome these obstacles. Women need each other more than ever when it comes to judgments about the future of our careers.

In talking to colleagues and mentors about promotion and tenure, be sure to pace yourself. Don't pester anyone with daily questions, and by no means don't email a colleague at 3:00 a.m. because you have a new idea about how to organize your teaching portfolio. Let colleagues know how you've acted on their advice. Being told "I took your advice" is even better than a thank you. Be sure to talk to your department chair regularly; at the very least make sure they know at the end of every semester how you're progressing toward tenure. It is essential that chairs understand your teaching experience and research goals, which might require explaining your research in some depth. Find out who has been on the department and institutional promotion and tenure (P&T) committees and ask their advice. You want to create the biggest support team possible. Ask all of them

- What does a successful candidate look like?
- What are the unwritten assumptions about what it takes to succeed?
- What are the pitfalls? What has caused people to be unsuccess-ful in the past?
- What do you look for during class visits?
- Would you walk me through your promotion package or teaching portfolio?
- Who has an exemplary package that you would recommend I ask to review?

Make good use of all the relationships you have been developing, and don't be shy about asking for advice. Wouldn't you be flattered if someone told you your materials were so exemplary that they should be a model for others?

Start collecting materials for your teaching portfolio as early as your first semester. Make a physical or electronic folder to collect copies of student assignments with your comments on them. Many people put an actual box in the corner of their offices to toss copies of assignments into, but you can also scan them into a folder on your desktop. Do whatever is easiest in compiling a bunch of examples that you can curate later to show your progress as an instructor. It is particularly effective if you have examples of early and later assignments that demonstrate improvement—both in your constructing of assignments and in your students' learning as a result of your feedback. Consider giving a pretest early in the semester to compare with the final. You won't be able to go back in time to obtain these artifacts when you need them. A colleague preparing her package for promotion to full tenure was shocked to discover that once students graduate, their work is deleted from our learning management system. I actually heard her screams from my office when she realized she only had the current semester's work to draw on. If you keep either hard or electronic copies of student work, then when you're preparing your package, you'll be able to flip through your collection to find the best examples for your portfolio.

Set up another electronic folder to store examples of assignments, exercises, labs, and active learning strategies you've designed as well as class notes. Keep copies of all the different things you create for class so you can sort through them later and pick out examples to show the variety of class materials you've created over the years. You might want to compare an early assignment you developed with its most recent iteration to reflect on how you have improved with experience. It will be much easier to go through folders set up for this purpose than to comb through all the class folders filled with irrelevant files when you are frantically trying to gather documents that demonstrate your teaching effectiveness.

Another thing you should start doing early on is figuring out what you'll need to take care of yourself. Become aware of the things you naturally do to self-calm so you can turn to them deliberately when your stress level gets so high you can't remember what to do. This applies to mind and body as well as to how you manage the project. For example, I find it helpful to make charts. This is particularly useful as a way to track where you are in the process. It gives me a sense of agency. You will be more productive if you have the resources to be thoughtful, creative, and patient. Take note of the things that make you feel more in control, and make a list you can consult if you start to feel panicky during the process. On another level, take a walk, slip into a bath, snuggle a pet or a willing human, play a video game, drink a glass of water, text a friend, delete old email, keep a gratitude journal. You get the idea.

The important thing is to do something deliberately: "I am going to do an hour of yoga in order to take care of myself." If you need a quick break, breathe in through your nose and out through your mouth a few times. This drives oxygen into your lungs and gives your brain a gentle jolt of stimulation. Whatever you do for yourself to manage the stress of preparing your package is going to be even more important to do after you submit your package. It's hard to believe when you are just getting started, but the most stressful time of all is when you're waiting for the decision. Ramp up the self-care during this period. You have just accomplished a huge milestone. Find a way to celebrate.

Because every place is different, I'm going to address three broad categories—service, research, and teaching—that will likely be a part of the process for everyone putting together a package to submit to a P&T committee. We'll start with service and research and then turn to teaching, the most complicated category to document (and for this reason is divided into multiple categories). We'll end with a few words about preparing your department chair to best support you.

Service

Every institution has different expectations and procedures, and at every one I have been at, junior faculty complain that the expectations are not clear enough. As Robert Boice bluntly explains in *Advice for New Faculty Members*, "Unstated and uncalibrated rules leave the most control for gatekeepers because they can adjust their implicit criteria to fit their biases" (203). This is a sobering observation. You are unlikely to get precise guidance on what demonstrates excellence in teaching, how many articles you need to publish, how much service you should contribute, or how long your teaching philosophy statement should be.

Make sure you understand the expectations as well as possible and know the procedures forwards and backwards. Ask someone who has recently been through the process to walk you through their experience. Believe me, people are usually happy to share, and reaching out builds your connection with colleagues—which is key to a successful tenure bid. You will be more likely to succeed if you have good relationships with the gatekeepers. You don't need to be friends with them, but they do need to see you as a productive and collegial member of the community. Try to find examples of what it looks like to be successful in each of the areas in your discipline. Here at the Naval Academy, for example, excellence in teaching is essential, and there are high expectations for research, but for tenure and promotion to associate professor, only minimal service is expected, such as advising students, participating in departmental committees, and generally being a good citizen. Institution-wide service is not the norm, although service is important for promotion to full professor. Beware! Service is frequently code for "congeniality," and this is a loaded category.

In too many cases, service means that you "fit in" with the department because you're just like those already there. If your department is dominated by older white men, this is going to be a challenge. Even departments that purposely hire to "diversify" the faculty too often balk at a diversity of experience and perspectives. Departments that just want to check the diversity box want us to look different but act just like them. Challenges to authority are too easily coded as "unprofessional." Tread carefully. I don't want you to stifle your voice or tell you to ignore an issue about which you feel passionate, but until you have tenure, you need to be aware that going toe to toe with someone who has influence over your future career is a risk you need to think carefully about taking.

There are other land mines hidden under the duty of service. You might, for example, be asked to do service and then be dinged for doing it because it took time away from your research. When you're asked to serve, use it as an opportunity to find out more about the assignment, committee structure, time commitment, expectations, outcomes, and assumptions that come along with it. It is always a good idea to express interest, to be flattered that you were considered, but also to say that you need to check with your chair first. If it's your chair who is asking, that can be tricky. You might feel comfortable saying that you need to discuss the scope of the obligation with your mentor or with the committee chair.

You might consider talking to your chair about creating a "service plan," in which you indicate the kind of service you're most interested in, such as curriculum or hiring. Not only will this look great in your tenure package, but it can also serve to remind a chair of all the things you've already taken on board. Chairs are human; they can forget that they have already asked you to do other things. A service plan is a good place to track your commitments and indicate your desire to contribute to the department. Be gracious if you have to decline, adding that you're looking forward to serving in just such a capacity after you make tenure. Some department cultures expect new faculty members to pick up the bulk of service assignments, while others carefully spare people from them. In the case of the latter, be watchful that your department doesn't protect you so well that you come up short on service in the eyes of the P&T committee. This is a good reason to talk to people from outside your department to clarify institutional expectations. In such a case, you might actually need to be proactive to get service assignments. Having a service plan is especially helpful in such situations.

Don't overwhelm the P&T committee with every little thing you've done for the institution, but do include all your departmental and institutional service assignments, including major one-off contributions and unassigned service you volunteered to do. For example, did you give a campus tour to a visiting candidate, speak to a departmental club about your research or job market experiences, write copy for a new course proposal, or step in to teach for a colleague whose children had stomach flu? All of these contributions show that you're a good colleague with the potential for institutional leadership—something that will be expected of you once you receive tenure.

Research

In the section on teaching, I will urge you to carefully curate your teaching portfolio to supply evidence of your teaching effectiveness without overwhelming the committee. Research, however, is where you want to overwhelm, but in a way they will easily register. In addition to providing a narrative in which you explain your research agenda—making sure to extend it past the tenure or promotion decision—consider including a chart of some sort that succinctly shows your progress and accomplishments. Following are two ways to do this, though you will likely have a vision of your own. The key is to be completely honest as well as comprehensive.

Directly below is a (totally made up) example of a table from Reilly Unluci, a physics professor, with the years forming the y-axis and the stage of the research in the x-axis. Notice how AY (academic year) 20 shows that there is work in the pipeline extending beyond the tenure date—projects just getting started, papers that have been submitted, and a grant that has been renewed. Since members of institutional P&T committees are usually from different disciplines, don't count on them to know what scholarship looks like in your field. This is especially true if you're a creative writer or visual or performing artist. Professor Unluci's narrative, for example, would need to include an explanation of what sorts of research activities are expected in her field (in this case, conference papers and journal articles), the lab she needed to set up to begin her research (and the effects on her research of having the lab destroyed by fire), and the significance of the grant she received.

Academic year	Start up	Launched	Completed	Submitted	Status
2015	Setting up lab			National Science Foundation grant	$800K awarded
2016	Documenting data lost after lab destroyed by fire			Conference paper 1	Grant deferred due to lab destruction No travel funds available for conferences
2017	Reconstructing lab	Data collection, project A		Conference papers 2 and 3	Grant reinstated Conference paper 1 delivered
2018		Data collection, projects B and C	Data analysis, projects A and B	Journal paper L Conference paper 4	Conference papers 2 and 3 published
2019		Data collection, project D	Data analysis, projects C and D	Revised and resubmitted journal paper X Journal paper M Conference papers 5 and 6	Journal paper X published Conference paper 4 published
2020		Data collection, projects E and F	Data analysis, project E	Journal paper N Conference papers 7 and 8	Grant renewed Journal papers M and N published Conference papers 5 and 6 published

The table below for Artemisia Standing, a French professor, has the academic years in the x-axis and the projects in the y-axis. It would be important for her to explain that in her field, monographs matter above all else, grants are nearly nonexistent, and journal articles and conference papers are primarily used to obtain feedback on book projects, with publishers expecting no more than three chapters of a monograph to have been previously published. She would also be wise to explain the long delays in the publication process, as one has to wait months after submitting an article to hear back from editors, the usual practice of asking an author to revise and resubmit, and the delay of months (and sometimes years) between acceptance and publication.

	Academic year 2015	Academic year 2016	Academic year 2017	Academic year 2018	Academic year 2019	Academic year 2020
Monograph (dissertation revision)	Revisions begun	Revisions completed	Submitted for publication	Revisions in response to editor	Accepted for publication	Published
Article 1	Submitted; revised and resubmitted	Accepted for publication	Published			
Article 2		Submitted	Accepted for publication	Published		
Article 3			Submitted	Revised and resubmitted	Published	
Conference paper A	Delivered at regional conference					
Conference paper B		Delivered at national conference				
Conference paper C			Delivered at society in my field			
Conference paper D				Delivered at international society in my field		
Five-year book project					Research begun	Drafting begun

Teaching

It is becoming more and more the norm for faculty to create teaching portfolios for job applications and promotion and tenure packages to provide evidence of their outstanding teaching. You may have already created one for your job search. Here at the Naval Academy, for example, even though teaching portfolios are not required, it is so common for tenure and promotion candidates to submit them that it seems odd when someone doesn't. We have moved to the online submission of all materials, which makes it even easier to create a teaching portfolio—but perhaps harder to create an effective one. While it's appealing to include everything you've ever created for all of your classes, resist the temptation. Your teaching portfolio should be carefully curated and impeccably organized. Make the master document concise, with hot links to supporting material. Organize your teaching portfolio so the committee can look at whatever they want—but knowing that the more there is, the less control you will have over what they choose to look at. Make sure there are multiple paths to key files, such as teaching evaluations. You do not want to have a committee member clicking around trying to remember where they saw the link to whatever they want to revisit. Ask your department chair to recommend exemplary teaching portfolios to use as a model, and ask your mentors to go through one of them with you so you can discuss what works best for you. Here are some of the categories you might use to organize your materials. Ignore those that don't apply, and add whatever additional categories you want:

- Diversity, equity, and inclusion statement
- Teaching philosophy (alternatively, teaching strategies or statement of teaching)
- Teaching responsibilities and goals
- Course materials and evidence of teaching effectiveness (syllabi, assignments, exams, projects, group work, innovations, etc.)
- Research with students (including student research you direct)

- Reflections on teaching and student evaluations
- Faculty development activities

Let's take a closer look at each of these categories.

Diversity, Equity, and Inclusion Statement

While there has been some controversy over the usefulness and appropriateness of statements of diversity, equity, and inclusion, they have become nearly ubiquitous. You likely wrote a diversity statement when you applied for your position. This is an opportunity to showcase all the invisible labor women and BIPOC men do in academia, which means you need to think hard about the contributions you have made that might not have been rewarded or commodified.

Consider the support you have given to students and colleagues as an informal mentor, for example. Think also about the mentoring and support you have received. If your institution has been welcoming and supportive, a statement is a great place to show your appreciation and commitment to joining that effort. Now is the time to align your own statement with your institution and department's diversity statements. This doesn't need to be long, and in fact, it shouldn't be, but it should have specific examples of what you've done in your teaching, research, and service to support diversity at your institution and in your discipline. You might want to include the diversity statement from your syllabus, for example. Consider the content of your courses and the way you teach in order to reach all of your students. How do you make your classes welcoming to everyone? What strategies do you use to connect with your students and foster an inclusive classroom community? What are your research goals? What service have you done, and what more do you plan to do? Decide how personal you want to be about your own intersectionality and how that impacts your experiences and work in academia.

Be sure to ask your mentors for advice and for examples of effective diversity statements. Your institution's affirmative action officer and diversity office are resources for you as you position your own beliefs in an institutional context. For a brief but balanced discussion of the concerns and advantages of diversity statements, read "More Colleges Are Asking Scholars for Diversity Statements. Here's What You Need to Know," an article by Sarah Brown in the *Chronicle of Higher Education*. It will also give you more ideas about how to construct your own.

Teaching Philosophy

Think of a teaching philosophy as an explanation of what you believe about how people learn. Most teaching philosophies I have read begin with a statement along these lines: "My philosophy of teaching is that students should be engaged in the classroom." It then goes on to talk about how you accomplish this engagement (but rarely discusses how engagement is measured). This is a goal you want to achieve, but it isn't a philosophy per se. What do you believe about learning that makes engagement important? The answer to that question should lead directly to what you therefore do to achieve and measure engagement.

There are schools of teaching that most of us never encounter outside the Education Department, but they exist. You do not have to invent the wheel, just figure out how you think it rolls. For example, I'm a constructivist. I believe that people learn by constructing their own understanding of the world. I design my classes so that students create their own knowledge. In my introduction to poetry class, we begin with several of Shakespeare's sonnets to see how he uses the form (or doesn't) in conjunction with the content. We read closely for structure and meaning, sometimes together and sometimes in small groups. Then the students write a sonnet of their own, so they can more fully understand what it feels like to work in the form. They are almost universally surprised at how difficult it is. They struggle with the rhyme scheme and even more so with the meter. I assess their learning by assigning a paper in which they analyze their own sonnet.

Take the 4 Sproles Tests of Educational Philosophy (4 STEP) Quiz (in "Workshops") to discover your teaching philosophy. While it is unlikely that you will fit squarely (or even mostly) into a single category, the quiz will help you define your teaching philosophy and provide you language to use in describing it in your philosophy statement. I hope the quiz gives you a sense of how to articulate what you believe about teaching and learning. After my writing partner, Irene Lietz, took the quiz, she wrote in an email to me,

> I find I am a constructivist but that I use critical pedagogy as an approach to accomplishing constructivist goals. I know the critical pedagogy is not necessarily student-centered or brain-based, but I believe critical pedagogy provides content and methods for engaging students in self-discovery and knowledge about the world and others that can challenge students to name their prior experience so that they can build on it in ways that will be useful and enlightening in their future lives. I have thought of myself as a critical pedagogist before but knew that I used active learning strategies like project-based learning to help students engage with their knowledge building. I don't find them mutually exclusive, but I do make constructivism primary. I was just surprised that I give priority to the constructivism.

Like Irene, most of the people who have taken the quiz get a score that puts them mostly in one category, but with answers falling into a second, third, or even fourth category. They are often surprised by this, but the goal is not to pigeonhole you; it's to help you describe your teaching philosophy and reflect on how that informs the choices you make about what you teach and how you teach it. For example, many quiz takers end up with a methodology in constructivism that complements critical pedagogy.

Regardless of your score, I think it is helpful to be able to be deliberate about the choices we make about what we teach and how we teach it. I hope the language in the quiz helps you define your own teaching philosophy. Remember, however, that you're writing your teaching philosophy for a committee that might not be familiar with your terminology. Be sure to write in a way that anyone from any discipline will understand.

Teaching Responsibilities and Goals

This is a relatively straightforward category that also allows you to expand on your vision for your teaching and your contributions to the institution and department. Remember that the P&T committee members may not be familiar with your department. It is important to help them understand how your offerings contribute to the department's mission.

Teaching responsibilities are best represented in a table that shows what you have taught over the past six or so years. You can include pertinent information about the courses such as enrollment and other things that matter to your institution, such as whether the course is required by the institution or the major, and whether it satisfies other graduation requirements. You can also include links to the course description, syllabuses, and student evaluations. Your goal is to make the information for the reviewing team as easy to read as possible. Following is a basic example from my early years of teaching to help illustrate how a table allowed me to discuss my larger teaching goals.

Fall 1987	Enrollment (68 total)	Requirement	Spring 1988	Enrollment (85 total)	Requirement
First-Year Composition	18	University	British Literature Survey II	45	English major
Shakespeare	25	English major	Medieval Literature	15	English major elective
Critical Theory	25	English major	What Do Women Want?	25	English major + women's studies elective

Fall 1988	Enrollment (88 total)		Spring 1989	Enrollment (85 total)	
First-Year Composition	18	University	British Literature Survey II	45	English major
British Literature Survey I	45	English major	Critical Theory	25	English major
Shakespeare	25	English major	Senior seminar: Virginia Woolf	15	English major + women's studies elective

Here is the statement of goals that would accompany this table:

> As you can see from this table, I teach a variety of courses that satisfy requirements for the university and for English and women's studies majors. While the English Department only has seven faculty members (one in composition and rhetoric, three in American literature, one in Classics, and two in British literature), we are committed to offering

courses that will give majors the broadest education in the discipline. Because my colleague in British literature focuses predominantly on Victorian poetry, I have created a three-year rotation of courses (What Do Women Want? British Literature and Feminist Theory, senior seminar on Virginia Woolf, and Lost Women: British Novelists) that provide English majors with a survey of British literature while also providing women's studies majors with the only electives in literature offered at the university. These courses thus serve a dual purpose and are particularly popular with a sizable number of students double majoring in English and women's studies. In addition to teaching courses required by the university and the department, it is my goal to offer a variety of courses, including Shakespeare and Medieval Literature, that will give students depth and breadth in British literature as well as a sophisticated understanding of feminist theory, which builds on the introduction they receive in this area in the required Critical Theory course.

This statement shows that not only had I held up my end by teaching courses the department needed, but also that I had developed a broader vision, represented by the courses I had developed to serve two different majors at the same time while also filling gaps in the department's course offerings.

Course Materials and Evidence of Teaching Effectiveness

The section on documenting your teaching effectiveness might seem like a straightforward category, but it requires selectivity to be persuasive. It also takes some planning and is one of the most important categories to get an early start on. For example, to demonstrate improvement, you might want to collect student writing samples from early in a course to compare with later ones. You might want to give a pretest early on in the semester to compare with the final exam. Remember that some learning management systems are tied to student email addresses, so if your institution doesn't allow students to keep their email after they've graduated, all their material will vanish along with them. Download examples of student work into a file to ensure that you have representative examples of student work for your teaching portfolio. Be sure to keep examples with your comments so that you can demonstrate your constructive feedback. You will of course want to include your rubrics.

As with your entire teaching portfolio, ask a trusted colleague to review this section to be sure that it is easily navigated and includes persuasive evidence of student learning. Again, remember that the entire committee won't be familiar with your discipline, so you should include introductions that explain the ways in which you are following, and innovating, disciplinary expectations.

Here are some of the things you might include in this section. In each case, select representative examples; don't overwhelm the committee with thousands of pages of everything you've done in class:

- Syllabuses—one for every course (not section) that you've taught; consider creating an introduction with the material you include in each syllabus, such as your statements on diversity, academic dishonesty, disability accommodations, and so forth
- Lecture notes and class plans
- Labs
- Quizzes
- Pre- and posttests
- Assignments and in-class exercises
- Student papers with your comments; consider creating a case study or two of students' writing that demonstrates how they improved over a series of drafts or over the course of the semester as a result of your feedback
- Exams
- Projects
- Group work
- Pedagogical innovations

It's a good idea to keep a file for each of the above categories and add to it every semester. You can then go back through them when you're compiling your teaching portfolio and select the best representative examples for each category. Make sure this section of your portfolio is easy to navigate. Create links to it from the other sections so the committee can quickly find examples that demonstrate your teaching effectiveness.

Research with Students

It's not necessary to have directed dissertations or honors projects to show that you've contributed to the research development of students in your department (but if you've done so, that's great). There are plenty of ways to promote student scholarship. This is the place to brag about your students' accomplishments, and the ways you've supported them.

Perhaps you've consistently attended to proper citation style and ethical research practices in your classes or you assigned students to read research in the field. Maybe you've taught students how to work as a team in ways that will prepare them to do collaborative research. Perhaps you've taken students to academic conferences or invited scholars to present their research to your classes. These are only some of the myriad ways to support and mentor student scholarship beyond supervising their projects.

I was challenged by doing research with students in my field—which doesn't naturally encourage collaborative research—until I began meeting weekly with English majors as a group to check their progress on honors projects, theses, and dissertations. I had been motivated to do this because of the number of students who had failed to complete their honors projects. I quickly saw the advantages of such a practice: it reduced their isolation, allowed them to learn from one another, cut down on time-consuming individual meetings, gave me a forum for explaining research strategies and mechanics once rather than multiple times, and provided the undergraduates with graduate student role models. Best of all, it helped me stay on task with my own research because of the threat of public humiliation if I had nothing to report each week.

Reflections on Teaching and Student Evaluations

In the annual workshop I hold on preparing for promotion and tenure, we spend the most time on how to frame student evaluations. Student evaluations are problematic: They don't measure student learning. They often ask questions students are not in a position to answer, such as whether the instructor covered appropriate material. How would they know? We've gone through all of this in Principle 6, but I'm going to repeat myself for the sake of putting reflection on teaching and student evaluations into the context of creating a teaching portfolio.

Student evaluations are an important part of evaluating an instructor's effectiveness on things only students would know, such as whether the instructor created a positive learning environment, was available for office hours, returned work in a timely manner, and provided constructive feedback. Unfortunately, student evaluations don't always focus on these things, and students are not typically given guidance on how to give constructive feedback. Too often they evaluations an opportunity for students to vent, especially when they're dissatisfied with the grades they've earned. Unfortunately, student evaluations make up the bulk—literally, in sheer volume—of what the P&T committee will read about your teaching. Given the amount of time it takes to wade through them, it's not surprising that they usually have an outsized influence. That's why you must frame them carefully and supply other sources of evidence about your teaching, including your colleagues' observations and your own reflections.

Principle 6 suggests that you reflect on your teaching and student evaluations. If you've done that each semester, this section will be a snap. If you supply the committee with a summary of the evaluations for each of your class sections, they might just send you flowers; committee members can spot check to ensure that the summary is accurate—or better yet, your chair can attest to the accuracy of your summaries—and save themselves hours of reading. Don't downplay negative comments; instead, interpret them. For example, this is the place to note that a cluster of negative comments stem from a section in which you exposed plagiarism. It is also the place to note implicit bias based on race and gender. You might need to educate the committee on this topic; do so gently but firmly, remembering to support your interpretation with outside evidence by quoting Principle 6 or other sources. Your reflection should note the modifications you made in response to student feedback and peer observations while also informing the committee about the probable cause for comments that ultimately didn't warrant any action on your part.

What your chair and the committee really want to see is that you've learned from experience and are likely to continue to do so. Making use of anything your teaching center or department offers in the nature of programs to gain insight into your teaching also demonstrates your commitment to continuous improvement. As I mentioned in Principle 6, if your campus doesn't have any such resources, work with your classes to provide mid-semester feedback—either by exchanging classes with a colleague to do a Formative Analysis of Classroom Teaching (described in the "Workshop" section) for each other or creating an anonymous poll in which you ask students what you should start, stop, and continue to do in class. Be sure to document the modifications you make based on the feedback you receive. Your reflection can then describe the progress you made in improving teaching over the years in the classroom. This is a powerful counterbalance to the student evaluations themselves.

Faculty Development Activities

This is an important category because it demonstrates your commitment to grow and improve as a teacher. Include books and articles you've read or written on teaching (including this one!), plus workshops and lectures you've attended or given, and don't forget the conference sessions you went to that focused on teaching. This will be an important category to populate as you go along, because you're likely to be doing so many things relevant to this category that you don't even notice how often you're taking steps to improve your teaching. If there's a Center for Teaching & Learning on campus, this would be a great resource for you. Attend their events, volunteer to lead discussions, take advantage of any mid-semester student feedback or peer observation programs offered, and document them in this section. If you can include brief notes on what you learned (or better) implemented, the more the better. These notes will help you later with your teaching philosophy statement and show consistency in your teaching practices.

Prepare Your Department Chair

As you're getting ready to go up for promotion or tenure, be sure to also prepare your department chair. Regardless of how involved the chair is in the tenure process, it's likely that at the very least the dean will consult with the chair about your candidacy. (This, by the way, is one reason why you want your chair to have a good working relationship with the dean.) Make sure your chair understands the contingencies you face in the department and in the classroom, especially if the chair has no experience of them. You might, for example, need to explain your students and colleagues' reaction to you if you're nonbinary. You might want to suggest that your chair read Kerry Ann Rockquemore and Tracey Laszloffy's *The Black Academic's Guide to Winning Tenure—without Losing Your Soul.* You might want to read it, too.

Ask your chair to review your materials with you early enough in the process to make revisions. Make sure your chair understands your research well enough to explain it to someone outside your discipline. Arm your chair with information about the appropriateness and competitiveness of journals and conferences where you have presented papers. Ask your chair to advise you on how to explain your contributions and value to the department. This will help ensure that the chair recognizes your contributions and value to the department and is invested in your narrative.

Even if your chair seems uninterested or too busy, schedule an appointment to deliver a one-page summary of your accomplishments at the end of the year. Inexperienced chairs might not realize the role they're about to play in your success. Gently guide them by giving them all the information they'll need to support you.

I hope you can see how all of the things we've covered up until now will play out in your bid for tenure and promotion, especially the connections you have made with your colleagues. Even if your department is not organized enough to help you through the tenure and promotion process, you can nudge them into supporting you by being proactive. Tell them how grateful you are for their support, and offer the same support to those coming up behind you; they're part of your network, too.

Once you've achieved tenure or promotion to full professor, celebrate your success, but not for too long. Many faculty find that the sense of relief after successfully completing the tenure process soon gives way to a feeling of purposelessness. I had a conversation with a colleague who after becoming full professor was having a hard time finding the motivation to continue his research. In his words, he felt he "no longer had anything to prove to the institution." You can avoid this crash by thinking past tenure and promotion as you plan your research agenda. Post-tenure is the time to ramp up your research, especially if you have a sabbatical. Now is the time to be bold in your research, for the sake of your career and for your next promotion to full professor. Don't stop once you make full: you're just hitting your stride as you consider the leadership roles you want to assume to make your institution the sort of place where you and other women can truly thrive. All this brings us to Principle 8, where you take the lead in imagining a revitalized academic culture.

How to Prepare for Promotion and Tenure

- Start preparing much earlier than you think you need to; your package needs to demonstrate your consistent track record of accomplishments in teaching, research, and service.
- Get advice from your colleagues, mentors, and department chair.
- Create a rich but concise teaching portfolio.
  - o Do some research on teaching philosophies for your own statement. (You can do this by taking the 4 STEP Quiz, in "Workshops.")

- o Collect evidence of the effectiveness of your teaching.
- o Frame your student evaluations. (Read Principle 6 for an extended discussion of how to do this.)
- o Balance student evaluations with peer observations, course material, and your own reflections and development.
- Present a clear and coherent research agenda and measurable accomplishments.
- Describe your contributions and value to the department in collegial service.
- Prepare your department chair.

Want to learn more? I recommend the following:

Brown, Sarah. "More Colleges Are Asking Scholars for Diversity Statements. Here's What You Need to Know."

Rockquemore, Kerry Ann, and Tracey Laszloffy. *The Black Academic's Guide to Winning Tenure—without Losing Your Soul.*

PRINCIPLE 9

Revolutionize the Culture of Higher Education through Generosity and Compassion

IN THE INTRODUCTION TO THIS BOOK, I asked you to imagine how the practical advice of the nine guiding principles could serve as the foundation for an inclusive and collaborative intellectual community founded on generosity, compassion, and a desire for us all to thrive. After reading the first eight principles, I hope you're beginning to see how to do for yourself what your institution won't do for you. Now I want to invite you to join me in imagining a new vision for the culture of higher education. It is a vision in which we can all thrive in our intersectional identities, fully embraced as we are—proudly gay, lesbian, bi, straight, trans, queer, cis, nonbinary, disabled, ablebodied, BIPOC, white, and none of the above.

In *Generous Thinking: A Radical Approach to Saving the University*, Kathleen Fitzpatrick imagines transforming higher education through structural changes: "Creating a more generous environment in which we can work together toward a new public commitment to higher education is going to require us all—from the individual level up through the institutional—to step outside the structures of competition into which we've been led and instead find new ways to approach problems together, in solidarity with one another" (232).

Fitzpatrick's argument would have institutions restructure to promote collaborative projects, reward service, and focus on the public good. In this same spirit, I am asking us to apply this kind of thinking at the individual level by being generous to one another. This would be good for us—and amazing for the students we teach. How do we transform higher education? By taking the lead and treating one another with compassion.

No matter your position—whether a graduate student, an adjunct, or a full professor—you have a leadership role at your institution. Lead up and lead down. When you reach out to colleagues, both junior and senior to you, you are a leader. When you accept and offer mentoring, you are a leader. Every day you stand before your students, you are a leader. You might not think of your scholarship as a leadership opportunity, but what are you doing if not taking the lead in your field? When you gently coach your chair to understand your tenure package, you are a leader. When a department meeting gets overheated and you suggest returning to the topic later in a calmer fashion, you are a leader. When you amplify another woman's voice to make sure she gets credit for her idea dismissed 10 minutes prior to a man suggesting the same thing to wild applause, what are you doing? Leading. In everything you do, you have a chance to model an attitude of generosity and compassion, something too often lacking in the culture of higher education. I think we should change that. It would be revolutionary.

Think of it. Every time you are thoughtful in expressing your anger in order to achieve a productive outcome, and every time you encourage a generous gesture, you are taking a leadership role that contributes to changing the campus culture. In my experience, the most entrenched divide is the impasse between faculty and administration. I have been on both sides of the division, and maintaining it seems like a surefire way to make sure nothing ever gets done. On a recent Zoom call with women in leadership roles from all over the country, one of them shared a story frequently punctuated by the explanation that the faculty's response was the result of how much everyone hated the provost. I don't think *everyone* hated me when I was provost, but the support I received came quietly and privately while the criticism was loud and public. It made me wonder why there is so often a rift between faculty and administration that creates a toxic climate on campus.

I think one reason is the objectification of the administration. When I served as a chair, I joked (sort of) that when a faculty member was upset about something—whether within or beyond my control— they would come into my office and yell at my desk chair. It wouldn't have mattered who was sitting behind my desk. A department chair is often treated like an actual chair. My joke has two points.

The first is not to take these attacks personally: they are aimed at your position, not you. This can be difficult to remember at times. The second is to acknowledge that not only does it feel awful to be the recipient of aggression, it also feels bad to be objectified. These diatribes constitute a double attack. Administrators often confide in me about such incidents. They wonder to themselves, "Don't they realize I'm the same person they once considered a trusted colleague?" Apparently not. A provost friend of mine described the ranting emails she receives as the faculty "yelling straight through me." I once refused a department chair's request because I was unable to grant it. He wouldn't accept no for an answer and made appointment after appointment to try to make his case. Each time, he brought more and more people with him, all of whom repeated the same argument. Finally, after three or four such meetings, in an attempt to restore civility, I said, "While I regret that I can't do as you ask, I have enjoyed talking with you all and getting to know more about your concerns." The chair replied, "If you enjoyed it, we haven't been doing it right."

These types of daily experiences are exhausting and time-consuming. If you've never spoken in anger to an administrator who holds a position you disagree with, it might be hard to imagine that such happens. If you have exploded with what you felt was justified, righteous indignation, you are still unlikely to realize how often it happens and how hurtful it can feel to the person on the receiving end.

I'm not sure how higher education came to draw this nearly universal battle line, but I've seen them develop. The administration needs to be supportive, encouraging, trusting, transparent, consistent, and attentive to listening to faculty and to communicating with them. All aspiring chairs, deans, and provosts, claim to possess these qualities. They know that these are the qualities a good administrator should have. Why do they so often not display them? Despite my good intentions, I repeatedly found myself in untenable situations. Pressure from the president and the board can put administrators crosswise with faculty. There might be pressure to quickly get things done, without lengthy consultation. There can be pressure to stand up to the faculty if they oppose something the president and the board want. There's also the experience of being played, which makes it hard to have trustworthy discussions with the camp that set you up. Sadly, I quickly learned to be suspicious of the line of petitioners who greeted me in the early days of a new position.

One memorable example of how trusting went wrong took place when I was a hired from outside an institution as a department chair. A number of faculty asked me again and again to create a faculty lounge for the department. This seemed like a perfectly reasonable request. The next time I met with the dean, who happened to be my predecessor, I was delighted to share that I thought I had figured out a way to rearrange the department office to accommodate the request. He nearly flew over the conference table in rage. The idea had apparently been a bone of contention for years. I walked right into it. I was never able to repair my relationship with the dean, a situation that didn't help the department in the long run. I have a long list of experiences that could have made me suspicious of faculty members—a feeling I urge administrators to resist. The faculty could be helped, however, if they had knowledge of why administrators might be prickly and defensive—such as the unpleasant situations they have to deal with but inevitably cannot talk about.

Among my unpleasant experiences as an administrator was having to address the issue of not one, but several, faculty predators who used their power in the classroom to groom students as emotional codependents or sexual partners. During the unfolding of one lawsuit, the entire contents of my office was subpoenaed. I would say more, but I'm under a gag order. It becomes difficult to trust your colleagues after seeing the damage such a thing can do to students. These are extreme examples, which perhaps make it easier to remember that one bad actor is not representative of the entire faculty. That said, administrators deal with all the bad actors, and that can easily taint their attitude toward the rest of us.

As an administrator, it was the petty irritations that more easily wore me down. I seemed to almost constantly be handling requests for special treatment, meaning that for financial reasons the same treatment typically couldn't be extended to everyone. I know that each rejection led the requester to resent me and often to speak ill of me. I also know that the special treatment denied was never shared as the reason for their often very personal criticism of me. Instead, I was accused of being unfair or playing favorites. The requests I disliked the most were the ones couched in principle, but clearly driven by self-interest. This seemed particularly malevolent, and the righteous indignation that accompanied such demands made them difficult to manage. "Is seniority worth nothing?" That's the question I heard when it came to almost everything, from pay raises to class schedules. It was easy to decipher this as code for "I should get special treatment." It can get to you after a while.

As an administrator, it's essential to remember that faculty members don't necessarily have an institutional perspective, and it's your job to help them see the bigger picture. It is also important to remember that administrative positions exist to head off the serious problems that do not, in fact, pervade the faculty but are isolated and unusual incidents—even when it seems like they occur many times a day. For every angry email, there are many, many more compassionate emails that people didn't take the time to write. It is hard to appreciate the absence of anger, but we must try. More to the point, we can change the culture by sending notes of gratitude and congratulations, by responding with understanding instead of frustration, and by trying to always see things from both perspectives.

I have watched warm-hearted and good-willed administrators quickly change as a result of a steady stream of angry and critical emails, public second-guessing, and berating, blaming them for making difficult decisions and for things over which they most likely have no control. I have seen administrators grow cynical about students as a result of having to deal exclusively with their complaints, problems, honor violations, and academic failures. Many administrators have described to me the loneliness that comes from being cut off from colleagues whom they thought were their friends. No matter how evil an administrator appears to be, it is unlikely they seek the destruction of the institution. They might define success differently than you, but I think it is safe to say that we all want our institutions to succeed.

I think the role of department chair is the most difficult. It certainly was for me. I did my best to help the department understand the dean's position, even as I tried to represent the department's position to the dean. I felt like the cobbler's bench I played with as a child—the toy where you pound wooden pegs into the outline of a shoe and then flip the bench over and pound them in again from the other side. At one point a dean pointed his finger at me and said, "Your problem is that you are a faculty advocate!" Stunned, I replied, "Yes. I am. That's my job." Apparently, that was another thing we didn't agree about.

The rift between faculty and administration can seem intractable, but I can't let myself believe that it is. Not only can we refuse to be part of the problem, we can also actively work against this culture of antagonism. We can do this in big ways and small, no matter our role at the institution. When a provost mentor of mine became president, I would get on her calendar for five minutes every month or so, just to bring her a latté. When another provost I knew sent out an email that I expected would incur pushback, I responded to it, "Great communicating. You rock!" I'm not suggesting these gestures transformed higher education, but if enough of us engaged in deliberately treating even those we most disagree with and dislike with kindness, respect, and generosity, I think it would be transformational.

The Arbinger Institute's *Leadership and Self-Deception: Getting Out of the Box* describes an organization committed to fostering self-awareness and growth by privileging collaboration over competition. During conflicts or impasses, individuals are asked to look to themselves for the source of the problem. It's called being in a "box." I recommend the book. I can't do justice to the practice of introspection it describes, but I'll cite an example of how it works for me.

You put yourself in a box when you do something you shouldn't have done, or more often, when you fail to do something you should have done. For me the signal is the voice in my head that says, If I were a good person, I would . . . work on this book; take out the trash; call an isolated friend; and so on. If I don't do one of these things, I'll go looking for excuses that exonerate me and put the blame elsewhere: "I would work on the book if I weren't so worn out from grading exams." This line of reasoning can quickly escalate into anything, from blaming students for not being prepared or listening or taking notes or taking the course seriously. I'm sure you've heard this conversation multiple times. It easily extends from blaming teaching online for students not performing as well as we think they should to blaming their performance on the lack of rigor in high school classes. Frustration with a class turns into a critique of the entire education system. I am so not to blame for that mess! It's one thing to blame an abstraction in pursuit of self-justification, but when we blame others, we begin to build a toxic environment. Blaming others to justify yourself can lead to

- Enjoying the failure of others and perhaps contributing to it by, say, withholding information.
- Encouraging others to help you build a culture of blame; have you noticed that your disgruntled colleagues tend to find one another and build a wall of hostility that blocks the possibility of collaboration or recognition of signs of goodwill?
- Trying to change others; if only so and so would stop being so obtuse!
- Objectifying others.

I have seen more people than I'd like to admit become bitter after a disappointment and build themselves a world of blame that festers from the inside and blights the world around them. It's easy to be critical of people who cast widespread blame to save face—The election was stolen! Immigrants are taking our jobs—but it's harder to see this pattern on a much smaller, personal level. You didn't get that job? Of course not; reverse discrimination makes it impossible for white men to succeed. They denied you tenure? Of course they did; the P&T committee is too ignorant to recognize gender bias in student evaluations!

I have seen people create alternative realities, conspiracy theories, and histories of their own martyrdom just so they could blame others for their situation, instead of accepting personal responsibility. I'm not suggesting that disappointments can't be absolutely crushing or even career ending. I'm just saying that a widespread structure of blaming students, colleagues, and, especially, administrators creates an intractable, toxic academic culture. Why would we want that?

You can get out of a box when you begin to see others as people with needs, hopes, and worries that are just as real as your own. It isn't easy, but if you stop objectifying whomever it is you're blaming, you begin to gain a perspective on the situation that allows you to foresee a productive solution, even if it means something as painful as acknowledging that your article does indeed need more work or that you aren't as well suited to your position or profession as you thought you were. This might sound simple, but it's actually hard. A big reason for the difficulty—and I hope you'll see how this fuels the divide between faculty and administrators—is that when you're in a box, your reaction tends to put the person you blame for your situation into their own box. If you're both in a box, there's no way out for either of you.

Several of my students got into a box after getting disappointing grades on their midterms. I was disheartened by their poor performance on this exam, which I thought they were prepped to ace. It was clear from the essays that many of the students had misunderstood or, more likely, hadn't read the material. They made embarrassing mistakes, like centering an essay around the death of Wordsworth's sister—who wasn't dead, as at the end of the poem he tells her to remember this moment in the future—or arguing that the message of Milton's poem about the drowning of an acquaintance is that we can conquer nature. I have no idea where these notions came from, because the students never pointed to any evidence from the poems to support these assumptions. That is the real reason for their lack of success. Of course, there isn't any evidence, but still.

So, for whatever reason, the students who got it all wrong were surprised that bluffing their way through the exam hadn't worked. Then, since they couldn't accept responsibility, they needed someone to blame: me. That's how they got into a box and how their behavior put me in a box as well. Here's an actual email I received from one of the students (with some details changed to protect those still in the learning process):

> Professor Sproles,
>
> I was surprised and deeply saddened by my grade on the twelve week exam. I feel as though there is some sort of miscommunication between my work and your grading because I am very passionate about my work and work very hard on it. I heavily analyze the poems we read and proofread the work I write, and I just feel as though my grade is not reflecting that at all. Most of the comments were just disagreeing with my ideas, not actual problems with my writing or analysis of quotes. I hope this does not come off as accusatory, as that is not my intention. I just do not believe I deserve low C's in your class. I hope we can meet to clear this up.

My initial response was to take offense. Grr! Your word against mine? While it's true that I disagreed with the student's reading of the poem, it was not my opinion that Wordsworth's sister still walked the earth. So how do I nudge this student from blaming me—and questioning the authority of a female professor—to doing the work of properly reading the poem and providing evidence for that reading? Good question. Do I humiliate the student by asking her for evidence of Dorothy Wordsworth's death in the poem and watch her fail away trying to find any? It would be tempting. Now, you can see, we are both in a box.

I shared the student's email with her advisor, a white male colleague, who said he had never gotten this sort of pushback from a student. He wrote back, "I wish had something to offer besides sympathy here. Obviously the facts are ALL on your side"—as if there were a debate. Seriously? My box just doubled in size. How could I respond to either of them in a way that would deescalate the non-debate? I knew I needed to help the student learn something, but really I just wanted to prove the correctness of my position: you don't get to insist that it's a matter of interpretation about whether a character is dead. Blah! I felt awful. I was so furious with both the student and my colleague that my eyes crossed. I still had to get myself and the student out of our boxes.

After I calmed down a bit, I tried to see things from the student's perspective—the first step in getting out of my box. She was embarrassed, both by the grade and most likely by her failed strategy of trying to pick up enough from the class discussion to bluff her way through the essay. It took some work to become semi-sympathetic, but I finally got out of my box. What I wrote back represented an attempt to get her out of her box by showing sympathy instead of taking offense: "I would love to meet. I, too, was disappointed in the grade you earned. Please know that I do not take off points if I disagree with an interpretation, only for factual errors and the absence of textual evidence. I understand that you are frustrated—that's because you care about literature. Let me know when you would like to talk."

When I saw her in class the next day, I said, "I am so happy to see you!" She was suddenly all smiles, and surprisingly responded, "I'm happy to see you, too." Now we were both out of the box. Reestablishing our friendly connection through my email and greeting paved the way for the conversation we needed to have. I know that she had lashed out at me because she couldn't face her own lack of preparation. Accusing her of that wouldn't have helped. She had to feel safe enough to see it for herself, and I needed to allow her to save face. I also needed to reject being objectified. I tried to bring my most compassionate self to our conversation, and I think it worked. When we had our talk, I said, "I think the problem is that we find out at the end of the poem that Wordsworth's sister has been there all along. I know that goes by quickly." This allowed her to save face: "Oh!" she said. "I missed that. I was wrong. I own that."

I can't guarantee that you'll always arrive at a happy ending, but once I was able to see the situation from the student's point of view, I was in a much better state to have this conversation. I think my change in attitude shifted the discussion so that it didn't become a full-blown argument. If I had instead said, "Show me in the poem where it says Wordsworth's sister is dead," and then sat back while she fumbled through it, digging deeper into her need to blame me, we would have spent the rest of the semester in our boxes. The Wordsworth incident led me to an important realization.

Because students tend to think that responses to literature are entirely subjective, when I point out a factual error—even though I simply write, "Where is the evidence for this?"—they think I'm disagreeing with their interpretation. Following my conversation with the student, I started writing, "I don't disagree with you, but you need to provide evidence from the text to support this claim." After that, my student evaluations for the first time included a number of comments like this one: "Poetry is all about interpretation, and Professor Sproles was very respectful of the fact that each poem will mean something different to each person. While she forced us to back our interpretations with textual evidence, she never shot down any ideas, perspectives or interpretations." We were most definitely out of the box.

Can you see how the dynamic caused by being in the box permeates higher education? If everyone hunkers down to defensively protect their own egos, no one is going anywhere. The boxes just get bigger.

I still vividly remember the revelatory moment of reading a novel in which a scene was described from one character's perspective and then from another's. The assumptions the first character had made—and that I was convinced were fully justified—turned out to be completely wrong. My nine-year-old brain exploded. I thought to myself, "The way I see things is different from the way my sister sees things. And different from the way my mother sees things. And the way my mother sees things is different from the way my father sees things. And then there's the way my teacher sees things." Suddenly the world got much bigger, and it became my new job to see all the perspectives possible. It's easy to lose sight of such revelations when you feel wronged, but that might be the best time to challenge yourself to imagine an alternative point of view. It's one way to stay out of the box.

Imagine a university where there's transparent decision making, where collaboration is rewarded, where competition is minimized, where coming onto campus makes you feel energized and even joyful. Imagine a place where leaders aren't afraid to make themselves vulnerable, to admit their mistakes, to pull the community together, and to trust that everyone is doing their best. Everyone would work for the good of the institution—not for personal or programmatic gain. People wouldn't avoid confrontation, but would instead work together to recognize and resolve their differences of opinion. People wouldn't be passive aggressive or objectify one another. Imagine how all this would change budgets, hiring, promotions, annual evaluations, class assignments, and even office space allocations.

When I teach women's studies, I always begin by asking the class to propose a set of ground rules for our discussions. They typically suggest that we respect one another, listen carefully, speak from experience, and uphold confidences. I also ask that we agree that everyone is doing their best. This is the hardest one for people to accept, but I insist that we talk it through: Isn't everyone trying their hardest? If we disagree, isn't it because we care? If someone says something that offends, isn't this a moment from which they can learn? If someone doesn't seem to be doing their best, shouldn't we try to figure out what's getting in their way? Are they lashing out to protect themselves? How can we help them save face? It's easier to be kind to people if you imagine that they're doing their best, knowing that you don't know enough about them to judge otherwise. That is what it means to be compassionate and generous. Don't you wish people would treat you that way?

Margaret Wheatley's *Turning to One Another: Simple Conversations to Restore Hope to the Future* begins, "I believe we can change the world if we start listening to one another" (7). Fitzpatrick sets out a similarly ambitious goal in *Generous Thinking*: "Listening is at the heart of the generosity I hope to inspire in the relationship between the university and the broader publics with which it interacts and on which it relies; generous listening is the necessary ground for generous thinking" (76–77). The complex and nuanced argument Fitzpatrick makes goes well beyond a foundation of listening. I urge you to read *Generous Thinking* for its vision of collaboration within academia and between higher education and the general public. Her description of conversations in which genuine listening occurs is exactly what Wheatley and I are striving for:

> Conversation imposes an obligation that cannot be easily concluded, that asks me to open myself again and again to what is taking place between us. Conversation thus demands not that we become more giving, but instead that we become more *receptive*. It requires us to participate, to be part of an exchange that is multidirectional. It disallows any tendency to declare our work concluded, or to disclaim further responsibility toward the other participants in our exchange. It asks us to inhabit a role that is not just about speaking but also about listening, taking in and considering what our conversational partners have to say, reflecting on the merits of their ideas and working toward a shared understanding that is something more than what each of us bears alone. (55; emphasis in original)

Fitzgerald is asking us to cast aside the academic culture of competition to create a collaborative intellectual community that sees disagreement as an opportunity for greater understanding rather than toxicity. I often think that when someone says the administration doesn't listen to the faculty, what they really mean is the administration isn't doing what they want them to do. If rather than accusing an objectified other of this or that we could engage in generous conversation, I think we could break through the all-too-common impasse between faculty and administration. I recently held a workshop on coaching for new student leaders that included an active listening exercise where I saw Fitzpatrick's vision in action. (You can find this exercise in "Workshops.") At the end of the exercise, I asked, "What did it feel like to be listened to?" One student responded, "It was refreshing!" Indeed, it is refreshing. What a perfect word to describe a feeling that's both novel and replenishing.

Wheatley's lovely book includes twelve suggestions for conversations that provide the perfect opportunity to listen deeply to one another by exploring questions like "What do I believe about others?" and "Can I be fearless?" I spent a year having these conversations with a group of deans and provosts. We met for lunch once a month and discussed one of the questions. We were a bit stiff at first, but soon enough we were having the most relaxing meetings I can recall. My goal was to help these administrators develop relationships with one another that went beyond the work of the institution. I hope the calm we also discovered continues to permeate their interactions with one another. I would like to see this peace envelop all of our colleges and universities. I recommend organizing similar conversations with your colleagues. It is hard to fall into a box with someone you're deeply listening to. It could be the start of an inclusive and collaborative intellectual community founded on generosity, compassion, and a desire for us all to thrive.

One final but essential point: be compassionate toward yourself. I have mentioned the importance of self-care before, but it deserves to be repeated. I'm serious; give yourself a break. I mean that in two ways. First, don't be so hard on yourself. You are doing your best, and if that isn't good enough for you, figure out what's getting in your way. Second, take some time off. It's best to get away, but even if all you can manage is a staycation, put an away message on your email and do something you enjoy for a day or more. Build breaks into your day. Whether you're following Boice's advice to take regular breaks during research or grabbing a quick nap, you will be more productive—and happier—if you can relax a bit throughout the day. I, for example, just spent 10 minutes searching for luxurious suites at the beach. What a lovely break! Fantasizing about relaxing is itself relaxing. One of my favorite tricks is to make my email password something that makes me happy. Amid a complex system of numbers and special characters, I insert periodic reminders to myself like "walking in London," "almost done" (with this book), or "baby Rhodes" (my daughter is expecting). Be deliberate about scattering reminders throughout your day of what makes you happy or calm or refreshed. The more compassion you show yourself, the easier it will be to show compassion to others.

How to Revolutionize the Culture of Higher Education through Generosity and Compassion

- Make an individual impact by being generous and compassionate.
- Resist the urge to objectify your colleagues.
- Recognize when you are in a box and get yourself out of it by seeing the other point of view.
- When someone is in a box, be compassionate, and instead of defending yourself, respond in a way that helps them out of the box.
- Assume that everyone is doing their best.
- Listen deeply to your colleagues.
- Be compassionate to yourself.

Want to learn more? I recommend the following:

Arbinger Institute. *Leadership and Self-Deception: Getting Out of the Box.*
Fitzpatrick, Kathleen. *Generous Thinking: A Radical Approach to Saving the University.*
Wheatley, Margaret J. *Turning to One Another: Simple Conversations to Restore Hope to the Future.*

CONCLUSION

___

Celebrate

IF YOU ARE LIKE ME, the minute you finish a project, a semester, or a milestone, you immediately move on to tackle the next goal. Always build in time to celebrate, however. Make it part of your timeline.

Organizing celebrations traditionally falls to women; it might be the one area in which there isn't a barrier against us. I think we should embrace this role. Before the pandemic, I threw a "Made It to May" party for new faculty, to celebrate their first year on the job. It was a celebration for all of us. I find it easier to organize celebrations for others than for myself, and if we celebrate one another, we multiply the joy. Hold a one-off discussion group to talk about a colleague's latest publication. Throw a book party and invite the bookstore to sell copies of a colleague's new book that can be autographed on the spot. Send notes of congratulations to everyone you know who received a promotion. Go out to lunch for birthdays. Do whatever you can to build community and connect your colleagues with one another.

In closing, don't forget to celebrate your contribution to a vision of higher education built on a foundation of generosity, collaboration, and compassion. Raise a glass of whatever you like best, and join me in a celebratory toast: You made it to the end of this book. Cheers!

WORKSHOPS

These are the workshops I referred to throughout the book. Some are geared toward faculty groups, a number are designed for the classroom, and others can be used for both classes and faculty workshops.

The 4 Sproles Tests of Educational Philosophy (4 STEP) Quiz

I wanted to find a quick way to introduce faculty to the various schools of teaching philosophies and at the same time help them understand more about their beliefs on teaching and learning. To do this, I created a four-question quiz on teaching philosophies so faculty can discover where they fit into these established categories. Because there are four answers to each question and participants are encouraged to select all that apply, the results are typically a combination of the four major philosophical schools of idealism (originating with Plato), pragmatism (originating with Aristotle), constructivism (originating with Jean Piaget), and critical pedagogy (originating with Paulo Freire).

I designed the quiz for use in workshops on preparing for promotion and tenure, but I discovered that all the faculty who've taken the quiz have been engaged by it as they discover more about themselves as teachers and are introduced (often for the first time) to established teaching philosophies in a way that is both approachable and applicable. You can take the quiz alone, with your mentor or mentee, in a one-hour workshop, or as part of a larger workshop. The following is an example of how a stand-alone workshop would work.

Workshop Agenda (60 minutes)

1. 10 min. Take the 4 STEP Quiz to identify your teaching philosophy. Note: The quiz is designed to allow participants to discover their teaching philosophy, which is often a a highly nuanced combination of the four primary philosophies: idealism, pragmatism, constructivism, and critical pedagogy.
2. 15 min. Working in pairs, discuss the teaching philosophy you arrived at based on the quiz; compile any questions you have about these philosophies.
3. 10 min. Share what you discovered: ask questions and offer comments about the 4 schools of teaching philosophies.
4. 15 min. Working in pairs, brainstorm examples of how your philosophy informs your teaching practice.

5. 10 min. Return to the larger group to share insights and ask further questions.

The 4 STEP Quiz

Directions: For each question, circle the item you agree with the most. If you are torn between answers, circle all those that resonate with you.

1. What is the primary purpose of education?
   a. To teach universal truths and promote intellectual development
   b. To develop a skilled and committed work force
   c. To guide students to challenge their own mental models and become thoughtful and active learners
   d. To teach critical thinking and to question traditional values so that students will become actively engaged citizens
2. What is the primary role of a teacher?
   a. To impart knowledge and values and model intellectual curiosity and mastery of the discipline
   b. To give students a solid foundation in a practical curriculum
   c. To create learning experiences that challenge students to create and reflect on their own knowledge
   d. To promote social change
3. What is the primary role of a student?
   a. To absorb knowledge
   b. To develop useful and practical skills
   c. To create their own meaning by engaging in learning experiences
   d. To become inspired to change the world by engaging in real-world challenges they care about
4. What is the most important thing to teach?
   a. Great works of Western civilization
   b. Basic skills, hard work, discipline, and respect for authority
   c. How to learn
   d. Social justice

Scoring: Add the number of responses you gave for each letter.
____a. Idealism
____b. Pragmatism
____c. Constructivism
____d. Critical pedagogy

The higher the number in a given category, the more inclined you are toward that particular teaching philosophy. Your answers might be spread over a couple of different categories or maybe evenly distributed among all four of them. If certain parts of a category resonate with you but others don't, just ignore the parts that don't fit your outlook. Remember: you're developing your own teaching philosophy. These categories will be helpful in giving you the language to create it.

Following is a bit of background on each of the four major philosophies, which you can mix and match to create your own teaching philosophy:

a. Idealism (also referred to as perennialism)
This philosophy traces back to the Greek philosopher Socrates (470–399 BCE) and his student Plato (ca. 428–348 BCE), who sought absolute truth. It values the life of the mind, and the great books and ideas of the Western tradition with an emphasis on literature, history, and philosophy. Its teaching practice tends to rely on teacher-centered pedagogy, such as lectures and chalk talks, but it also encourages discussion.

If you want to read more about idealism, see Mortimer Adler and Charles Van Doren, *How to Read a Book: The Classic Guide to Intellectual Reading*, or Allan Bloom, *The Closing of the American Mind: How Higher Education Has Failed Democracy and Impoverished the Souls of Today's Students*.

b. Pragmatism (also referred to as realism or essentialism)
This philosophy traces back to the Greek philosopher Aristotle (384–322 BCE), who was taught by Plato, and his search for unmediated reality. It values the physical world and emphasizes a common knowledge of the basics, especially in mathematics and the physical sciences. Its teaching practice tends to rely on teacher-centered pedagogy, such as lectures, chalk talks, and labs that students observe and replicate.

If you want to read more about pragmatism, see E. D. Hirsch Jr., *Cultural Literacy: What Every American Needs to Know* or *How to Educate a Citizen: The Power of Shared Knowledge to Unify a Nation*.

c. Constructivism (also referred to as progressivism; closely connected to brain-based learning, which strictly speaking is not a teaching philosophy)
This philosophy traces back to Swiss biologist Jean Piaget (1896–1980) and was further developed by Russian psychologist Lev Vygotsky (1896–1934). It postulates that learners construct their understanding of the world by developing mental models that hold until challenged. Its teaching practice insists on student-centered learning experiences that engage students in creating their own knowledge. The science of brain-based learning supports constructivist pedagogy by showing that the process of cognitive development relies on the internal creation of new knowledge.

If you want to read more about constructivism, see Lev Vygotsky, *Mind in Society: The Development of Higher Psychological Processes*; also explore Ernst von Glasersfeld's website (http://vonglasersfeld.com). For more on brain-based learning, see Susan Ambrose et al., *How Learning Works: 7 Research-Based Principles for Smart Teaching*, and James Lang, *Small Teaching: Everyday Lessons from the Science of Learning*.

d. Critical Pedagogy (also referred to as reconstructionism)
This philosophy traces back to Brazilian educator Paulo Freire (1921–97), who argued that education was not the same as "banking" information, but is instead a practice for liberating through social change those oppressed by classism, racism, and misogyny. Unlike the Aristotelian belief that objective reality is the object of study, critical pedagogy holds that reality is subjectively constructed by each individual within a social context. It takes a critical look at knowledge production, asking who decides what counts as knowledge and how decisions are made about what gets taught. Like constructivism, critical pedagogy teaching practice insists on student-centered learning experiences that engage students in interrogating the social and political world. Feminist pedagogy has its foundations in Freire's work.

If you want to learn more, see Paulo Freire, *Pedagogy of the Oppressed*, or Henry Giroux, *On Critical Pedagogy*. I also recommend bell hooks, *Teaching to Transgress: Education as the Practice of Freedom*.

Formative Analysis of Classroom Teaching (FACT)

I didn't invent Formative Analysis of Classroom Teaching (FACT), but I did come up with the name: Don't just make guesses about how to improve your classes, rely on the FACT. I learned the process from Carol Hurney, associate provost for faculty development and director of the Center for Teaching and Learning at Colby College, who brought it to James Madison University from the University of Virginia, but I think it's used all over the place. I have learned more about teaching from conducting FACTs than from anything else. FACTs are a quick, impactful way to gather anonymous mid-semester feedback from students by having another faculty member, who is trained as a FACT consultant, take over your class for the last 15 minutes and you leave the room. There is a more detailed description below, but first here's a quick overview of the process.

The consultant begins by explaining the importance of the student evaluations completed at the end of the semester. It is important to state this because students typically don't know that their evaluations are used to make promotion and tenure decisions about faculty. When I ask students what they think happens to the forms after they turn them in, they say the faculty member reads them, but they don't realize they have any function beyond this. After explaining how many people will be reading their evaluations and the impact they have on faculty members, the consultant explains that the FACT is different: it is anonymous on their part, and for the instructor is confidential. Also, because it's done mid-semester, it can have an immediate impact on the course.

Students divide up into small groups; it is best to have at least three groups, but the FACT is scalable. I have done FACTs for groups of up to 500 students. The consultant asks the groups to brainstorm about their learning in the class: What helps them learn? What hinders their learning? What suggestions do they have for the instructor? They all list their ideas in a shared Google doc, and then the consultant asks a student to read the three aloud, during which the consultant makes sure to understand them. This has the additional benefit of allowing the students to discuss the comments with one another—which is the real advantage of the FACT over an instructor collecting their own mid-semester feedback.

The students often help one another better understand what's happening in the course. In a math class, for example, one group of students was furious that the questions on quizzes and seemed to come out of nowhere, without prior class preparation. To that, another student replied, "You aren't doing the homework, are you?" The complaining group erased their comment. It has so much more impact when clarification comes from a classmate. During the discussion, students can use an asterisk (*) to identify comments with which they strongly agree and a caret (^) to indicate comments with which they strongly disagree. This gives the instructor a clear sense of the extent to which a comment represents the feelings of the class.

At the end of the FACT, the consultant copies the Google doc into another file, so the names of the writers can't be traced, and shares it with the instructor in a meeting, at which time they can also discuss what the class said. The one-on-one can be a rich discussion of pedagogy and of the class, since the consultant was privy to the small-group discussions as well as to what the students wrote. In the final stage of the FACT, the instructor talks to the class about changes that can possibly be made based on the students' comments. This discussion is also an opportunity to clarify misconceptions and to explain why some things can't be changed. My students inevitably suggest that we read less—the idea often being that we strike the longest reading assignment on the ground that the book is irrelevant or unrelatable. It's wonderful to have an opportunity to talk to them about why that assignment is an important part of the course.

If you don't already have FACT on your campus, I recommend you start it yourself. You only need one other colleague, and then you can do them for one another.

Benefits of FACT

Value to Faculty Members

- Provides timely feedback that can be addressed immediately
- Allows for immediate correction of misunderstandings
- Demonstrates to the students your commitment to teaching and respect for students
- Provides an opportunity to talk about teaching with a colleague, who has the potential to become a mentor
- Provides information that can be used for reflecting on teaching and inclusion in your teaching portfolio for promotion and tenure

Value to Students

- Increases engagement in the class
- Contributes to greater and more sophisticated understanding of pedagogical choices
- Provides an opportunity to call out unproductive peer behavior
- Allows students to see that it can be beneficial to them if faculty are alerted to something that isn't helping them learn

Value to the Institution

- Offers a robust institution-wide structure of support to faculty
- Creates community among faculty members, including a community of faculty consultants
- Allows faculty to meet colleagues and find mentors outside of their disciplines
- Builds bridges within an office of academic affairs and across the institution
- Demonstrates to students and to faculty that a commitment to teaching is a fundamental part of the institution

Below are the results of a FACT that I conducted with 170 student tutors.

Top 10 Helps

- Well-structured instructor notes and handouts
- Practice problems

- Visual aids
- Multiple specific examples
- Group work/peer instruction
- Well-prepared and well-paced lessons
- Clear syllabus and learning objectives
- Homework with solutions provided later
- Interactive teaching/engaging students
- Practice tests and quizzes

Top 10 Hindrances
- No clear learning objectives/lesson plans
- Extensive lectures without breaks
- Excessive homework
- Unnecessary derivations and no context for equations
- Not using the textbook content
- Problems with online homework
- Death by PowerPoint
- Instructors not available or helpful
- Instructors not engaging students
- Distractions in class by other students and technology

Top 10 Suggestions
- Interactive teaching/engaging students
- Clear syllabus and objectives
- Group work/peer instruction
- Practice test/exams
- Appropriate amount of homework with solutions provided later
- Instructor handouts and student notes
- Course evaluations and progress reports
- Appropriate pace
- Provide multiple examples and concepts
- Use textbook questions and clicker questions

About FACTs

FACT Goal
The goal of the FACT process is to assist faculty members with their own reflective teaching by providing them with anonymous mid-semester feedback from their students. FACT results should be confidential, with no records retained by the facilitators.

FACT Timing
A FACT is conducted mid-semester, after students have received at least one grade but with enough of the semester left for the possibility of changes being made.

FACT Request
A FACT is appropriate for any faculty member who practices (or who wishes to practice) reflective teaching. Because the FACT provides information faculty members can use for reflection and self-assessment, it must be requested by the faculty member. A FACT is not effective if it's recommended or required.

FACT Consultants
FACT consultants are trained by requesting a FACT, observing a FACT, and conducting a FACT under observation. Consultants gather at the beginning and end of each academic year to discuss and assess the program, sharing insights, observations, and suggestions.

FACT Process
After a faculty member requests a FACT, a trained consultant, who is a faculty member from a different department or division, is assigned to conduct the FACT. There are several reasons for having the consultant be from a different discipline (although I have known of the process being conducted within a department). I think it is helpful if the consultant knows very little about the subject of the class because that makes them less likely to impose their own judgment or think to themselves, "I would teach this by doing X, Y, and Z." The consultant's role is just to transmit the students' comments to the instructor and be available for a conversation about teaching should the instructor wish to have one.

After a faculty member and a consultant agree to conduct a FACT, the consultant arranges to visit one of the faculty member's classes, usually during the last 15 minutes. The faculty member leaves the classroom, after which the consultant explains how student evaluations are used (especially for tenure and promotion) and then goes over the FACT process. The consultant asks the students to work in groups of three to six to discuss their learning in the class.

Getting students organized into groups is perhaps the biggest challenge for the consultant, depending on the configuration of the room and whether the students are used to doing group work. My biggest tip for a room with fixed seating is to have the front row turn around to face the second row, and then I divided the two rows into groups of four or six. When all else fails, I've had the students stand up and cluster in the aisles. As I've mentioned, I did a FACT for 500 students in an auditorium, and it worked; the key was having a lot of consultants along with me to herd the students into groups. I asked the first row to stand and face the second row, and so on. We pulled students into the aisles to give the students in the middle of the rows a bit more space. It was pretty chaotic, but everyone had fun, and we got amazing feedback.

Each group brainstorms ways in which their learning is helped or hindered and suggestions they have for changes to enhance their learning. Responses are recorded in a Google doc that the consultant has shared with the class. After the responses are recorded, the consultant invites students to put an asterisk (*) next to the comments with which they strongly agree and a caret (^) next to the comments with which they disagree. The consultant asks a student to read the comments aloud, pausing for discussion. The consultant asks the students to explain their responses if they are unclear, and this conversation frequently leads to a lively discussion in which students help one another better understand the pedagogical choices that the instructor has made for the class.

The consultant subsequently meets with the faculty member for a 30-minute conversation to deliver the results, which have been copied into another file to prevent tracing the comments back to individual students. The consultant's role is simply to be a spokesperson for the students, thus allowing them to remain anonymous. The consultant's role is not to evaluate the class or the faculty member; suggestions should never be offered unless explicitly requested. The conversation between the consultant and the faculty member is also an opportunity for colleagues to talk together about teaching. Consultants often report that they feel they learn as much or more than the faculty members from the process. The consultant gives the single copy of the FACT results to the faculty member. That is the end of the consultant's role in the process.

FACT consultants agree to maintain triple confidentiality: not to identify individual students to the faculty member; not to discuss the results of a FACT in any way that would identify the faculty member; and not to initiate future discussion about the FACT with the faculty member (although they will welcome further conversation if it is initiated by the faculty member).

The conversation between the consultant and faculty member should occur prior to the next class meeting so the faculty member can immediately discuss the results with the class. Students invest a great deal in this process and look forward to the faculty member's response. Closing the loop by discussing the results with the class is an essential element—perhaps the most important element—in this process. It is a must that the faculty member, at the very least, acknowledges the comments the students have made. Ideally, the faculty member will begin the next class after the FACT with a discussion of the class's suggestions, including how they will be implemented or why they cannot. This is also an opportunity to clear up any misconceptions or confusion students may have.

The FACT is an extremely useful tool in the self-assessment of teaching, and faculty members are encouraged to include their reflections on those from the FACT in their annual reports. It is worth reiterating that FACT consultants are not evaluators. They are not to report any information about a FACT to anyone other than the faculty member requesting the FACT, whose results and requesting faculty member should be kept in the strictest confidence. No records of any kind should be retained, and no information reported. On the other hand, the faculty member who requests the FACT is encouraged to discuss the FACT process, its results, and the reflections it produces as they wish. Their reflection affords an opportunity for conversation with colleagues, chairs, deans, and other individuals who may be in a position to evaluate the faculty member. Faculty members are also encouraged to continue to contact the consultant who conducted their FACT for further conversations about teaching.

The Game of 35

The Game of 35? Because that's the highest possible score possible, but more about that in a minute. I didn't invent this game, and I don't know who did. I have found instructions for it, but none of them cite a source. If you know who invented it, let me know. Beware that it's noisy and a bit chaotic. I like that—it feels like a cocktail party. Once the class has played it once, it goes very fast the next time; it takes maybe 10 minutes, and best of all, it scales beautifully. In fact, the larger the group, the better. I've played it with a group of 75. It really primes a class to participate for the rest of the semester, so I use it on the first day of class to create learning objectives. I'm sure there is a way to do this online. Let me know if you figure one out.

The Game of 35 is a great ice breaker for any class or workshop, but it is much more than that. It also generates ideas and creates collaborations to construct student-centered knowledge. By the end of the game, students have had five discussions on the topic and are ready to have a robust follow-up discussion. It is also a quick and fun way to establish consensus. The best way to explain how it works is to play it.

The Rules

Let's start with some sample questions for the class or workshop to consider in a round of the game:

- What do you hope to get from this class/workshop?
- What is the primary thing you hope to learn in this class?
- What should be the main focus of this class/workshop? (E.g., in a workshop on time management, I start with a Game of 35 by asking, "What, besides not having enough of it, is your biggest problem with time?")
- At the end of a class/workshop you can ask, "What is your number one takeaway from the class/workshop?" or "What are you still confused about / want to know more about?"
- How would you define X, with X being a complex term or concept? (Note: Asking for a simple definition does not work well.)
  o What are the primary characteristics of modernism?
  o How would you define academic dishonesty?
  o What is a key component of a statement on diversity, equity, and inclusion?

After a question is selected, the participants will formulate an answer and then everyone else will rank the responses based on their general agreement with the answer or statement.

Let's get started.

1. The instructor or group leader asks a question or provides a prompt, and students write a response to on an index card. The students then swap cards with a partner. Two rules of the game are that the students never see their own card again or rate the same card more than once.
2. Everyone finds another partner, and together they compare the two cards they hold. There are seven points available to distribute between the two cards, and the partners must agree on how to allocate them, with no fractions allowed. If the pair thinks the cards are equally good, one would get a 4 and the other a 3. If the pair really doesn't agree with one of the cards, it might get a 0 and the other card a 7.
3. After deciding on the point allocations, the students write them on the back of the card.
4. Next, the students find a new partner and exchange cards— remembering never to rate a card more than once—and again discuss answers and allocate points. They repeat the process until each card has five scores; they then add them up.
5. The card with the highest score represents the consensus of the group.

A perfect score is 35, but I have never seen a card receive one. I always ask if anyone has a card with 35; then I ask if anyone has one over 25. If no one has a card with a score over 25, I ask if there are any over 20. I usually take the top three or four scores and add them to the syllabus, create a class statement on academic dishonesty, or establish goals for a workshop. I also ask if anyone has a particularly interesting card we should consider. If I use the game to establish workshop goals or learning objectives, I make sure to come back to them periodically for an assessment of how we're doing.

Mentoring, Coaching, and Active Listening

Clearly these three connected topics deserve more than one workshop. It takes years of experience and practice to develop the skills required. Mentoring doesn't necessarily lead to coaching, but if a mentee requests help with a problem, coaching skills will come in handy. If you're interested in developing your coaching skills, I highly recommend "Coaching for Greater Effectiveness," a workshop by the Center for Creative Leadership. I've participated in the center's version of the active listening exercise below. It's a good idea to create a transition between mentoring (where you share your experiences) and coaching (where you're helping your mentee arrive at a solution to a problem). Ask your mentee, "Would you like some coaching on this?" During mentoring and coaching, active listening is the most important thing a mentor does.

A workshop that asks participants to consider their own experiences of mentoring and being mentored is a great way to help people in both positions be more deliberate about mentoring practices. It can be done within a department as well as institution wide. The following guidelines provide bullet points for prompting discussion and serve as a quick reference when you need a refresher. The active listening exercise is great for mentor-mentee pairs.

Mentoring

Definition: Mentors offer guidance based on their personal experience. Mentors are not experts; they just have relevant life experience to draw on. Mentors offer emotional support to those in new and challenging situations.

4 Steps to Mentoring
1. Build a relationship and develop trust.
   - Plan to spend 10 or 15 minutes with your mentee every week
   - Be willing to share your experiences, but limit venting and complaining
   - Show interest and concern by asking your mentee about her background, family, pets, teaching, research, and generally how things are going; find something you have in common
   - Instead of asking "Do you have any questions I can answer?" say "I know you must have lots of questions; maybe I can help answer some of them"
   - Maintain confidentiality
2. Listen actively.
   - Pay attention to body language—leaning forward and nodding your head show you are listening
   - Ask open-ended (rather than yes/no) questions
   - Ask probing questions: "Tell me more about your classes"
   - Ask for clarification
   - Repeat back what your mentee says to ensure that you understand an important issue
   - Be aware of the emotions coming through in the conversation
3. Don't give unsolicited advice.
4. Do offer to coach your mentee through challenges, but don't insist.

Coaching

Definition: The goal of coaching is to help someone find a solution to a problem or challenge.

Coaches give only the gentlest of advice. Primarily, they listen and ask questions until a solution emerges.

Stages of Coaching
1. Build the relationship
2. Learn the details of the situation—be sure to use active listening
3. Ask questions that will get your mentee to question assumptions about the situation
4. Offer your support but also help identify other sources of support
5. Set goals (with dates for completion) for resolving the issue

Active Listening: An Exercise

This exercise is designed for groups of four, but it can be modified for groups of different sizes by reducing or increasing the number of things to listen for. I did this exercise at the Center for Creative Leadership's "Coaching for Greater Effectiveness" workshop. It was an awesome experience to feel deeply heard.

Instructions

Form groups of four. Read the instructions all the way through and then begin.

1. Figure out whose middle name comes first alphabetically. That person is #1. The person sitting to their right is #2, and so on.
2. Person #1 speaks first, sharing with the group a specific example of something that has been challenging for them. (2 minutes).
3. Person #2 summarizes what person #1 just said (1 minute).
4. Person #3 shares the emotions that came through in what person #1 said (1 minute).
5. Person #4 shares the values that came through in what person #1 said (1 minute). Person #4 is also the timekeeper. Each person should be allowed to finish a sentence before being interrupting but be sure to keep the group on track so everyone can share a challenge.
6. Person #1 shares how it felt to experience active listening (1 minute).
7. *Now*, person #1 becomes #2, person #2 becomes #3, and so on.
8. Repeat the exercise until everyone has had a chance to play every position.

When you're coaching someone, you should be listening for content, emotion, and values. After you've listened, tell them, "This is what I heard you saying: [summary] . . . Is that right?"

Planning a Realistic Summer Break

You can do this exercise on your own, with your mentor or mentees, as a 50-minute workshop or as part of a larger workshop. I use it at the end of the "Planning for Promotion and Tenure" workshop to help participants better visualize what they need to do every day between the workshop and the day their tenure applications are due. I also do it with the group of new faculty that I meet with weekly during their first year. For that group, I also do a version for the winter and spring breaks.

If you're doing this exercise in a group, I ask everyone to share their long-term goals with the group after part I, then we do parts II and III and share the plan with a partner, who then becomes the natural choice for the accountability partner selected in part IV.

Participants begin by reflecting on their long-term goals. The end date they select might be a milestone like tenure/promotion or it might be whatever number of years they're able to see into the future. After listing the goals they hope to complete, they fill in the chart between the current year and the year by which they hope to fulfill those goals by establishing the yearly goals they'll need to meet in order to make their deadline. This exercise sets them up to better understand what they will need to accomplish during the coming summer break. That exercise often leads people to adjust their long-term timelines, which are often either unrealistic or insufficiently ambitious.

With the summer stretched out in front of you, it's easy to feel like you have all the time in the world. This exercise will help you see that you have less time than you think, and likely more plans than you can fit into the break. This is the time to be realistic about what you can accomplish and to be sure to schedule some downtime so you start the fall semester refreshed instead of already harried and feeling behind.

The Template

Here is the template I use for this exercise. It's important to have a space for each day of the break. I'm giving you the start of the template for summer, but you can easily reduce the number of spaces to make this work for fall, Thanksgiving, winter, or spring breaks.

Part 1: Career Goals
1. What would you be most disappointed about not having achieved five to ten years from now?

2. In the next five years/by the next milestone (e.g., dissertation defense/tenure/promotion/retirement), I hope to have achieved the following goals:
   -
   -
   -
   -
3. Long-term plan (Work your way up from today, at the bottom, to the milestone date, at the top, sketching out a timeline for achieving the goals you listed above.)

   MILESTONE DATE: _____

   TODAY

Part 2: One-Year Goals Timeline
Fill in the timeline with intermediate deadlines that will need to be met

May	Aug (classes begin)	Dec (grades due)	Jan (classes begin)

Part 3: Summer Break Timeline
1. Map out what you will need to do in order to meet your goals for the summer.
2. In your timeline, be sure to include vacations and travel plans, time with family and friends, course planning (make notes now, but don't work on courses until August). Also be sure to allow time for colleagues to review your research prior to submitting it for publication.
3. Find a research partner and schedule a weekly coffee date, email, or phone check-in to gauge your progress and, if necessary, revise your plan.

4. The plan begins on the last day of classes, because it's important to capture the time you have during finals week, when you're waiting to give exams or receive research papers.

FRIDAY: LAST DAY OF CLASS

MONDAY

MONDAY

And so on—you get the idea—until classes begin again.

5. Goals for fall:
-
-
-
-
-

Part 4: Accountability Partners
Find a partner and schedule a weekly check-in either in person or via email or virtually.

You will be surprised at how effective having someone you're accountable to can be. Don't feel like you can't change your plans or report that you haven't accomplished as much as you had hoped. Having a plan will help you see what modifications you need to make to meet your long-term goals. It will also allow you to celebrate the incremental victories you achieve along the way.

Stereotype Threat: How to Mitigate It in the Classroom

I developed this handout for a reading group on Claude Steele's *Whistling Vivaldi: How Stereotypes Affect Us and What We Can Do.* I compiled examples from the book for use in the classroom to mitigate stereotype threat. Definition: When a person tries to avoid falling into an internalized (often unconscious) stereotype—such as women aren't good at math or BIPOC people aren't good in school—the added stress this creates can cause that person to be less successful—thus proving the stereotype. This is particularly problematic during high-stakes tests.

The following are ways to mitigate stereotype threat in the classroom. The bullet points can be used to spark discussion or as a refresher.

- Assure students that race and gender are not a factor for success, and make sure they aren't.
- Give lots of low-stakes assignments instead of a few high-stakes exams or papers.
- Lower anxiety levels by giving assessments low-stakes names; e.g., "reading checks" or "scavenger hunts" instead of quizzes.
- Lower test anxiety by giving open-book exams.
- Focus on the process rather than just getting the right answer.
- Allow for resubmissions of work.
- Make sure students have enough time to complete in-class assessments; remember that they cannot work nearly as fast as you can.
- Encourage women and BIPOC students to consider graduate school.
- Mentor your women and BIPOC graduate students.

REFERENCES

Adler, Mortimer, and Charles Van Doren. *How to Read a Book: The Classic Guide to Intellectual Reading.* Touchstone, 1972.

Ambrose, Susan, Michael Bridges, Michelle DiPietro, Marsha C. Lovett, and Marie K. Norman. *How Learning Works: 7 Research-Based Principles for Smart Teaching.* Jossey-Bass, 2010.

Arbinger Institute. *Leadership and Self-Deception: Getting Out of the Box.* Berrett-Koehler Publishers, 2018.

Bain, Ken. *What the Best College Teachers Do.* Harvard University Press, 2004.

Baumeister, Roy F., and John Tierney. *Willpower: Rediscovering the Greatest Human Strength.* Penguin, 2012.

Bloom, Allan. *The Closing of the American Mind: How Higher Education Has Failed Democracy and Impoverished the Souls of Today's Students.* Simon and Schuster, 1987.

Boice, Robert. *Advice for New Faculty Members: Nihil Nimus.* Pearson, 2000.

Brent, Rebecca, and Richard Felder. "A Protocol for Peer Review of Teaching." *Proceedings of the 2004 American Society for Engineering Education Annual Conference & Exposition.* Session 3530. American Society for Engineering Education, 2004.

———. *Teaching and Learning STEM: A Practical Guide.* Jossey-Bass, 2016.

Brown, Austin Channing. *I'm Still Here: Black Dignity in a World Made for Whiteness.* Convergent, 2018.

Brown, Sarah. "More Colleges Are Asking Scholars for Diversity Statements. Here's What You Need to Know." *Chronicle of Higher Education*, January 29, 2019.

Cain, Susan. *Quiet: The Power of Introverts in a World That Can't Stop Talking.* Broadway Books, 2013.

Center for Creative Leadership. ccl.org.

Chodorow, Nancy. *The Reproduction of Mothering: Psychoanalysis and Sociology of Gender.* University of California Press, 1978.

Clance, Pauline Rose, and Suzanne Imes. "The Imposter Phenomenon in High Achieving Women: Dynamics and Therapeutic Intervention." *Psychotherapy: Theory, Research & Practice* 15, no. 3 (1978): 1–8.

Covey, Steven R. *7 Habits of Highly Effective People: Powerful Lessons in Personal Change.* Simon and Schuster, 2020.

Daut, Marlene L. "Becoming Full Professor While Black." *Chronicle of Higher Education*, July 28, 2019. https://www.chronicle.com/article/becoming-full -professor-while-black/.

Dweck, Carol. *Mindset: The New Psychology of Success*. Ballantine Books, 2007.

Eagly, Alice H., and Linda L. Carli. *Through the Labyrinth: The Truth about How Women Become Leaders*. Harvard Business Review Press, 2007.

Fitzpatrick, Kathleen. *Generous Thinking: A Radical Approach to Saving the University*. Johns Hopkins University Press, 2019.

Friedrickson, Barbara. *Positivity*. Harmony, 2009.

Freire, Paulo. *Pedagogy of the Oppressed*. Penguin, 2017.

Germano, William, and Kit Nicholls. *Syllabus: The Remarkable, Unremarkable Document That Changes Everything*. Princeton University Press, 2020.

Giroux, Henry. *On Critical Pedagogy*. Bloomsbury Academic, 2020.

Goleman, Daniel. *Focus: The Hidden Driver of Excellence*. Harper, 2015.

Gray, Tara. *Publish and Flourish: Become a Prolific Scholar*. Teaching Academy, New Mexico State University, 2005.

Gurung, Regan A. R., and Noelle R. Galardi. "Syllabus Tone, More Than Mental Health Statements, Influence Intentions to Seek Help." *Teaching of Psychology*, February 11, 2021. https://journals.sagepub.com/doi/10.1177 /0098628321994632.

Hall, Roberta, and Bernice Sandler. "The Classroom Climate: A Chilly One for Women?" Project on the Status and Education of Women, Association of American Colleges, 1982.

Hawks, Matt. "The Daily Question: Building Student Trust and Interest in Your Course." Presented at the United States Naval Academy's Third Annual Conference on Teaching and Learning, Annapolis, MD, May 15, 2018. https:// www.usna.edu/CTL/_files/documents/3rd_Annual_Conference/Hawks _Questions_CTL_conf.pdf.

HERS (Higher Education Resource Services): Women Leaders in Higher Education. hersnetwork.org.

Hiatt, Gina. "Why Writing Productively Is So Difficult, and What to Do about It." *PMLA* 133, no. 1 (2018): 179–85.

Hirsch, E. D., Jr. *Cultural Literacy: What Every American Needs to Know*. Vintage, 1988.

———. *How to Educate a Citizen: The Power of Shared Knowledge to Unify a Nation*. Harper, 2020.

hooks, bell. *Teaching to Transgress: Education as the Practice of Freedom*. Routledge, 1994.

Jaffe, Eric. "Why Wait? The Science behind Procrastination." *Observer*, March 29, 2013.

Johnson, W. Brad. *On Being a Mentor: A Guide for Higher Education Faculty*. 2nd ed. Routledge, 2016.

Johnson, W. Brad, and David Smith. "Mentoring Someone with Impostor Syndrome." *Harvard Business Review*, February 22, 2019. https://hbr.org/2019 /02/mentoring-someone-with-imposter-syndrome.

Kreitzer, Rebecca J., and Jennie Sweet-Cushman. "Evaluating Student Evalua-
    tions of Teaching: A Review of Measurement and Equity Bias in SETs and
    Recommendations for Ethical Reform." *Journal of Academic Ethics* 1, no. 12
    (2021). https://doi.org/10.1007/s10805-021-09400-w.
Kuh, George. *High-Impact Educational Practices: What They Are, Who Has Access to
    Them, and Why They Matter.* AAC&U, 2008.
Lang, James. "The Promising Syllabus." *Chronicle of Higher Education,* August 28,
    2006.
———. *Small Teaching: Everyday Lessons from the Science of Learning.* Jossey-Bass,
    2016.
Manne, Kate. *Down Girl: The Logic of Misogyny.* Oxford University Press, 2018.
McGonigal, Jane. "The Game That Can Give You 10 Extra Years of Life." TED-
    Global, 2012. https://www.ted.com/talks/jane_mcgonigal_the_game_that
    _can_give_you_10_extra_years_of_life/transcript?language=en.
———. "Our Puny Human Brains Are Terrible at Thinking about the Future: And
    That Has Consequences." *Slate,* April 13, 2017.
———. *SuperBetter: The Power of Living Gamefully.* Penguin, 2016.
Mitchell, Koritha. "Good Teachers Know That Bodies Matter." *Public Books.org,*
    November 3, 2021. https://www.publicbooks.org/good-teachers-know-that
    -bodies-matter/?utm_content=buffer47c81&utm_medium=social&utm
    _source=twitter.com&utm_campaign=buffer&fbclid=IwAR2WDxsGMrr2oyS
    aogy4BR7qDPANTlRrK3229Ev4ETIuWQiYmG5EIoWOxAE.
Naudé, Johan, and Florence Plessier. *Becoming a Leader-Coach: A Step-by-Step
    Guide to Developing Your People.* CCL Press, 2014.
Nelson, Trisalyn, and Jessica Early, "How to Counter the Isolation of Academic
    Life." *Chronicle of Higher Education,* February 3, 2020.
Neuhaus, Jessamyn. *Geeky Pedagogy: A Guide for Intellectuals, Introverts, and Nerds
    Who Want to Be Effective Teachers.* West Virginia University Press, 2019.
Niemann, Yolanda Flores, Gabriella Gutiérrez y Muhs, and Carmen G. González,
    eds. *Presumed Incompetent: The Intersections of Race and Class for Women in
    Academia.* Utah State University Press, 2012.
———. *Presumed Incompetent II: Race, Class, Power, and Resistance of Women in
    Academia.* Utah State University Press, 2020.
Pirtle, Whitney N. Laster. "Motherhood While Black: The Hard Truth about Race
    and Parenthood." In "The Awakening: Women and Power in the Academy."
    Chronicle of Higher Education, April 6, 2018.
Pitcher, Erich. *Being and Becoming Professionally Other: Identities, Voices, and
    Experiences of U.S. Trans* Academics.* Peter Lang, 2018.
Price, Christy. "Why Don't My Students Think I'm Groovy? The New 'Rs' for
    Engaging Millennial Learners." *Millennial Traits and Teaching: The Teaching
    Professor,* August/September 2009.
Revuluri, Sindhumathi. "How to Overcome Impostor Syndrome." *Chronicle of
    Higher Education,* October 4, 2018. https://www.chronicle.com/article/how-to
    -overcome-impostor-syndrome/.

Rockquemore, Kerry Ann, and Tracey Laszloffy. *The Black Academic's Guide to Winning Tenure—without Losing Your Soul*. Lynne Rienner Publishers, 2008.

Russo, Richard. *Straight Man*. Vintage, 1997.

Sandberg, Sheryl, with Nell Scovell. *Lean In: Women, Work, and the Will to Lead*. Deckle Edge, 2013.

Silva, Paul. *How to Write a Lot: A Practical Guide to Productive Academic Writing*. APA LifeTools, 2007.

Sproles, Karyn. "The Emotional Balancing Act of Teaching: A Burnout Recovery Plan." In *Teaching and Emotion*, ed. Harriet L. Schwartz and Jennifer Snyder-Duch. New Directions for Teaching and Learning 153. Wiley, 2018.

———. "To Write a Different Story: Reflective Reading as a Pedagogical Practice of Restorative Justice for Racial Oppression." In *Reflective Reading and the Power of Narrative: Producing the Reading*. Routledge, 2019.

Steele, Claude. *Whistling Vivaldi: How Stereotypes Affect Us and What We Can Do*. Norton, 2011.

Steinhorst, Carl, with Jonathan McKee, *Can I Have Your Attention? Inspiring Better Work Habits, Focusing Your Team, and Getting Stuff Done in the Constantly Connected Workplace*. Wiley, 2017.

Tannen, Deborah. *You're Wearing That? Understanding Mothers and Daughters in Conversation*. Ballentine, 2006.

Vosniadou, Stella, and William F. Brewer. "Mental Models of the Earth: A Study of Conceptual Change in Childhood." *Cognitive Psychology* 24, no. 2 (October 1992): 535–85.

Vygotsky, Lev. *Mind in Society: The Development of Higher Psychological Processes*. Harvard University Press. 1978.

Weimer, Maryellen. *Learner-Centered Teaching: Five Key Changes to Practice*. Jossey-Bass, 2013.

Wheatley, Margaret J. *Turning to One Another: Simple Conversations to Restore Hope to the Future*. Berrett-Koehler Publishers. 2009.

INDEX

ABO: Women in the Arts, 33
academic culture: competitive nature, 3, 127–28, 133; departmental, 105; revitalization, 120, 122–36
academic department chairs, 23–25; as faculty advocates, 127; impostor syndrome in, 14; relationship with new faculty, 22; service work and, 105; student evaluations and, 77–78, 85; tenure and promotion process involvement, 101, 119–20, 121
academic departments, 23, 24–25, 27, 104–5, 112–14, 121; staff, relationships with, 22, 27
academic honesty, 69
Academic Ladder Inc., 96
Academic Writing Club, 96
accountability groups/partners/strategies, 32–33, 51–52, 91, 94–97, 99, 155, 157–58
active learning, 56–61, 70, 71, 102, 112
adjunct faculty, 16, 19–20, 33, 123
advice: colleagues as source of, 21–22. *See also* mentors/mentoring
affinity groups, 24, 25, 26
affirmative action officers, 110
Ambrose, Susan, *How Learning Works: 7 Research-Based Principles for Smart Teaching*, 57
amygdala hijack, 49–50, 53
antiracist cohorts, 25
anxiety: grades-related, 83; impostor syndrome-related, 3, 6, 10, 65, 83; introversion-related, 20; stereotype threat-related, 4–5, 65, 158; writing-related, 95
Arbinger Institute, *Leadership and Self-Deception: Getting Out of the Box*, 127–28

assistant professors, 17, 100
associate professors, 100, 104
authority, challenges to, 105; from colleagues, 82; impostor syndrome, 3, 4, 6–7; misogyny and racism, 61, 101; from students, 61–64, 130. *See also* subject expertise

Bain, Ken, *What the Best College Teachers Do*, 67–68
Baumeister, Roy, *Willpower: Rediscovering the Greatest Human Strength*, 48–49, 98
Bennett, Linda, 36
bias, gender or racial, 19; of mentors, 28–31; of student evaluations, 40, 61–62, 64, 77–84, 87, 118; in tenure and promotion process, 104
BIPOC (Black, Indigenous, people of color) faculty, 4, 19, 24, 29, 31; student bias toward, 61–62, 77–78
BIPOC female faculty, 5–6, 9–10, 19, 25, 29, 32, 61, 81; student bias toward, 40, 62, 77, 84, 87
BIPOC individuals, stereotypes, 4–5
BIPOC students, 41, 62–63, 91
BIPOC women, 3, 6
Black faculty. *See* BIPOC (Black, Indigenous, people of color) faculty
blame: for administrative decisions, 126–27; as "in the box" mindset, 127–33
body language, 36, 153
Boice, Robert, *Advice for New Faculty Members*, 12–13, 19, 44, 53, 90, 92, 93, 95, 96–97, 104; "Let Go of Negative Thoughts," 98
brain-based learning, 59, 94
breaks: in daily routine, 135; summer and winter, 40, 46, 51, 53, 55, 139, 154–57, 155

breathing exercises, 48, 50

Brent, Rebecca, 40, 85–86

Brewer, William, "Mental Models of the Earth," 56–57

brief daily sessions (BDS), 13, 38, 53, 93, 95–96

Brown, Austin Channing, *I'm Still Here: Black Dignity in a World Made for Whiteness*, 25

Brown, Sarah, "More Colleges Are Asking Scholars for Diversity Statements," 110–11

burnout, 55–56

Cain, Susan, *Quiet: The Power of Introverts in a World That Can't Stop Talking*, 20–21

Carli, Linda, *Through the Labyrinth: The Truth about How Women Become Leaders*, 43–44

Carnegie, Dale, *How to Win Friends and Influence People*, 21

celebration, of accomplishments, 137

Center for Creative Leadership, Coaching for Greater Effectiveness workshop, 38–39

centers for teaching and learning, 22–23, 118–19

cheating, 69, 76

childcare, 43–44, 45, 47, 92, 101

Chodorow, Nancy, *The Reproduction of Mothering*, 80

Chronicle of Higher Education, 3, 59, 111

Clance, Pauline, "The Impostor Syndrome in High Achieving Women," 3, 6–7

clothing, 9–11

coaching, 40, 42; workshops, 38–39, 134–35, 139, 152–54

collaboration, 116, 122–23, 127–28, 133, 134, 137

colleagues: of adjunct faculty, 19–20; bias of, 19; connections with, 16–27, 33, 127; as friends, 24–25, 27, 127; mutual mentoring relationships, 30–31, 32–34; peer class observations, 40–41, 77, 85–86; support for female and BIPOC faculty, 62; tenure and promotion preparation and, 101, 120

collegiality, 19, 23–24

communication: active listening skills, 133–35, 136; conversations with colleagues, 20, 25–26, 34; in mentoring, 36–37

companionship, professional, 41

compassion: in culture of higher education, 122, 123, 126, 133, 135, 136, 137; toward oneself, 135–36; toward students, 71, 74, 131; as women's attribute, 80; in work relationships, 41

competition, 3, 122, 127–28, 133, 134

conferences, 26, 28–29, 89, 107–8, 116, 119

confidentiality, 37, 149, 153

conflict resolution, 127–28, 133

congeniality, 104

constructivism, 56–57, 61, 111, 112, 143–44

continuous improvement, 118

contract renewal process, 23

Covey, Steven, *7 Habits of Highly Effective People*, 45, 46–47, 52

COVID-19 pandemic, 20, 33, 67, 95, 137

credibility, 3, 51, 77–78, 81

culture, of character or personality, 20–21. *See also* academic culture

curriculum, new courses, 54–55

curriculum vitae (CV), colleagues' review of, 34

Daily Question, 69–70

Daut, Marlene L., "Becoming Full Professor While Black," 77

deadlines, 95, 156, 158

decision fatigue, 48–49, 53

decision making, 48–49, 126–27, 133

discussion pairs, 67

dissertation committees, 89

dissertation directors, 26, 29, 32, 116

dissertations, 18, 29, 35, 52, 88, 108, 156

distraction, 48

diversity, equity, and inclusion statements, 109, 110–11, 115

diversity, within departments, 104–5

diversity office, 110

Dweck, Carol, *Mindset: The New Psychology of Success*, 7–8, 9, 11

Eagly, Alice, *Through the Labyrinth: The Truth about How Women Become Leaders*, 43–44

identity: contingencies, 4–5; intersectional, 61, 69, 110, 122; LGBTQ+, 25; stereotype threat and, 64–66; of students, 60–61, 64, 65–66; teaching and scholarship in relation to, 64, 88, 90

Imes, Suzanne, "The Impostor Syndrome in High Achieving Women," 3, 6–7

impostor syndrome, 1–15; fixed mindset and, 7–9, 10; leadership roles and, 14; stereotype threat and, 4–6

inadequacy, feelings of. *See* impostor syndrome

inclusivity, 39, 122

institutional structure, 122–23

"in the box" mindset, 127–33, 136

introverts/introversion, 16, 20, 21, 24, 27, 67, 70

Jaffe, Eric, "Why Wait? The Science behind Procrastination," 47

Johnson, Tori, 52, 97–98

Johnson, W. Brad, *On Being a Mentor: A Guide for Higher Education Faculty*, 3, 15, 29–30

Judge, Carolyn, 96–97

judgments/judging, 17; fixed mindset and, 7–8, 11, 12; impostor syndrome and, 1, 3, 4, 5, 9–11, 15; by mentors, 31; by students, 61–62. *See also* student evaluations

junior faculty, guidelines for success, 12–13

Kreitzer, Rebecca J., "Evaluating Student Evaluations of Teaching," 84

Kuh, George, 66

Lang, James: *Small Teaching: Everyday Lessons from the Science of Learning*, 57, 58–59; "The Promising Syllabus," 67–68

Laszloffy, Tracey, *Black Academic's Guide to Winning Tenure—without Losing Your Soul*, 77–78, 119

Latina faculty, 30

leadership, 8, 14, 21, 35–36, 38–39, 64, 82, 106, 120, 123–24, 133

learning management systems, 102, 114

lectures, 55, 58, 69, 70, 118, 143, 147

letters of recommendation, 28, 46

LGBTQ+ faculty, 24, 25, 31

LGBTQ+ students, 61

Lietz, Irene, 29–30, 52–53, 94–95, 112

lifelong learners, 91

listening skills: active listening, 133–35, 136, 154; in mentoring, 36–37

Manne, Kate, *Down Girl: The Logic of Misogyny*, 69, 80

Massoni, Kelley, 80

maternity leave, 32

mathematics, 4–5, 65, 143, 145, 158

McGonigal, Jane, 47–48; *SuperBetter: The Power of Living Gamefully*, 50–51, 53

meetings, 23, 35, 37

memory, long-term and short-term, 58–60

Mentoring, Coaching, and Active Listening workshop, 139, 152–54

mentoring communities, 33

mentors/mentoring, 3, 24, 28–42; cited in teaching portfolio, 110; division-wide program, 39–41; formal, 31–32; gender and racial biases, 28–31, 32; horizontal (peer), 30–31, 32–35, 36–37, 41; impostor syndrome and, 3, 15, 37; micro-mentoring sessions, 37, 42; potential mentors, 25, 27, 35–36, 41; promotion and tenure preparation and, 101; of students, 41, 42; vertical, 30; workshops, 36, 134–35, 139, 152–54

mindfulness, 48, 50, 53

misogyny, 69, 77, 78, 80, 83, 84, 101, 144

Mitchell, Koritha, "Good Teachers Know That Bodies Matter," 61

Molloy, John, *Dress for Success*, 21

monographs, 107–8

Montoya, Liliana Velasquez, 52

motherhood, 80–81

mother transference, negative, 80–81, 82, 83–84

National Center for Health Statistics, 6

Naudé, Johan, *Becoming a Leader-Coach*, 38–39

Nelson, Trisalyn, "How to Counter the Isolation of Academic Life," 26

networks, 16, 22–23, 26, 27, 94, 120

Neuhaus, Jessamyn, *Geeky Pedagogy*, 60–61, 64

new faculty: avoidance of research, 89; connections with colleagues, 16–27;

mentoring program, 39-41; orientation, 22-23, 24; social isolation, 17-19. *See also Advice for New Faculty Members* (Boice)

Nicholls, Kit, *Syllabus: The Remarkable, Unremarkable Document That Changes Everything*, 61

Niemann, Yolanda Flores, 62

nonbinary faculty, 24, 25, 29, 31, 119

objectification, 124, 128, 133, 136

O'Brien, Rich, 39-41

old boys' club, 30, 32, 33

online teaching, 16, 65-67, 69, 128, 147

parental leave, 45, 79

Peart, Silvia, 57-58

peer observations, 77, 118-19; paired, 40-41, 85-86

peer review, 60, 76, 91

physical appearance, 9-10, 80

Piaget, Jean, 56-57, 58, 143

Pirtle, Whitney N. Lester, 6

Pitcher, Erich, *Being and Becoming Professionally Other: Identities, Voices, and Experiences of U.S. Trans* Academics*, 25

plagiarism, 76, 117-18

Planning a Realistic Summer Break workshop, 40, 46, 51, 53, 139, 154-57

Plessier, Florence, *Becoming a Leader-Coach*, 38-39

poems and poetry, 63, 68, 74-75, 111, 114, 129-32

power differentials, 31, 37

"Preparing for P&T" workshop, 73

Price, Christy, "Why Don't My Students Think I'm Groovy?," 66

prioritization, 45-47, 53

problem solving, 8, 94

procrastination, 47-48

promotion: colleagues' support during, 19; failure in, 8-9; reviews, 9-10. *See also* tenure and promotion process

provosts, 36, 76, 123-24, 125, 127, 135

publications: delays in, 108; failure in, 8-9; mentors' assistance with, 28-29; rejection, 97-98; for tenure, 89

racism, 4-5, 32, 77, 79, 101, 144. *See also* bias, gender or racial

reappointment, colleagues' support during, 19

recruitment, of BIPOC or female faculty, 29, 39-41

research/scholarship, 88-99; accountability in, 91, 94-97, 99; balance with service work, 105; career path and, 89-90; charts and tables of, 106-8; of colleagues, 24; feedback on, 16-17, 96-97, 99; as habit, 88-99; as leadership opportunity, 123; partners or groups, 24; post-tenure, 120; preparation time, 46; rejection, 97-98; with students, 90-91, 109, 116; sustaining, 38; as teaching portfolio component, 106-8

resiliency, 50-51, 53

retention, of faculty, 40-41

Revuluri, Sindhumathi, "How to Overcome Impostor Syndrome," 6

Rockquemore, Kerry Ann, *Black Academic's Guide to Winning Tenure—without Losing Your Soul*, 77-78

role models, 116

Ross, Mary Alice, 30, 53

Russo, Richard, *Straight Man*, 23

sabbaticals, 120

Safe Space / Safe Zone trainings, 25

Sandberg, Sheryl, *Lean In*, 35

scavenger hunts, 67-68

scholarships, 36

self-affirmation, 10-11, 13, 15

self-awareness, 127-28

self-care, 103, 135-36

self-criticism, internalized, 10, 13

self-help books, 21

self-talk, negative, 10-11, 13, 15

self-worth, 9

senior faculty, 19, 31-32, 82, 83-84

service plans, 105

service work, 19, 29, 34, 100, 103, 104-6, 110, 121, 122-23

Shaffer, Jason, 30

Skipper, Daphne, 94

Slate, 47-48

small-group work, 59-60

Smith, David G., 3, 15

social anxiety, 20

social isolation, 17-19, 27

Tierney, John, *Willpower: Rediscovering the Greatest Human Strength*, 48–49, 98

time management, 43–53; brief daily sessions (BDS), 13, 38, 53, 93, 95–96; in promotion or tenure preparation, 101; of research and writing time, 88, 91–96, 99

transgender faculty, 25

unconscious mind, 94

University of California, Berkeley, 50–51

University of Southern Indiana, 36

US Naval Academy, 8, 26, 39–41, 49, 63, 70, 84, 104, 109

Vosniadou, Stella, "Mental Models of the Earth," 56–57

Weimer, Maryellen, *Learner-Centered Teaching: Five Keys to Practice*, 59–60

Wheatley, Margaret, *Turning to One Another: Simple Conversations to Restore Hope to the Future*, 133–34, 135

White, Judith, 36

women, stereotypes, 4–6

women faculty, 19, 41

Wordsworth, William, "Tintern Abbey," 74–75

workday, 23–24

work-life balance, 43–53, 89, 91–92

writing, 1–2, 90; accountability groups/ partners, 29–30, 33, 91, 94–96, 99. *See also* publications

Zoom, 22, 33, 63, 67, 123